DEATH
AND
DESIRE

LITERARY
CURRENTS
IN
BIBLICAL
INTERPRETATION

EDITORS

Danna Nolan Fewell
Perkins School of Theology,
Southern Methodist University, Dallas TX
David M. Gunn
Columbia Theological Seminary, Decatur GA

EDITORIAL ADVISORY BOARD

DEATH
AND
DESIRE

the rhetoric
of gender
in the
apocalypse
of john

T I N A   P I P P I N

•

WESTMINSTER/JOHN KNOX PRESS
Louisville, Kentucky

DEATH AND DESIRE:
THE RHETORIC OF GENDER IN THE APOCALYPSE OF JOHN

© 1992 Tina Pippin

First edition

Published by Westminster/John Knox Press,
Louisville, Kentucky

This book is printed on acid-free paper that meets the American National Standards Institute Z39.48 standard. ∞

PRINTED IN THE UNITED STATES OF AMERICA
2 4 6 8 9 7 5 3 1

Library of Congress Cataloging-in-Publication Data

Pippin, Tina, 1956-
  Death and desire : the rhetoric of gender in the Apocalypse of John / Tina Pippin. — 1st ed.
      p.   cm. — (Literary currents in biblical interpretation)
  Includes bibliographical references and indexes.
  ISBN 0-664-25157-9 (alk. paper)

  1. Bible. N.T. Revelation—Criticism, interpretation, etc. 2. Women in the Bible. 3. Death. 4. Desire. I. Title. II. Series.
BS2825.2.P56 1992
228'.06—dc20   92-30723

For Jerry

ACKNOWLEDGMENTS

Parts of chapters 3, 5 and 6 appear in a different form in *Searching the Scriptures: A Feminist-Ecumenical Commentary*, ed. Elisabeth Schüssler Fiorenza, New York: Crossroad. Reprinted by permission of the Crossroad Publishing Company.

"Fire and Ice," by Robert Frost, is from *The Poetry of Robert Frost*, ed. Edward Connery Lathem, copyright © 1951 Robert Frost. Reprinted by permission of Henry Holt and Company Inc.

CONTENTS

Series Preface 9
Preface 11

1 · Introduction:
Desiring Apocalypse 15

2 · The Politics of the End of the World:
Method and Madness 25

3 · An Apocalypse of Women:
Subverting Catastrophe 45

4 · The (W)hor(e)ror of It All:
The Ideology of Death 57

5 · Fantasy and the Female:
The Ideology of Desire 69

6 · Conclusion:
The Endless End of the World 87

Notes 111
Bibliography 117
Indexes 129
Illustrations 133

SERIES
PREFACE

New currents in biblical interpretation are emerging. Questions about origins—authors, intentions, settings—and stages of composition are giving way to questions about the literary qualities of the Bible, the play of its language, the coherence of its final form, and the relations between text and readers.

Such literary criticism is rapidly acquiring sophistication as it learns from major developments in secular critical theory, especially in understanding the instability of language and the key role of readers in the production of meaning. Biblical critics are being called to recognize that a plurality of readings is an inevitable and legitimate consequence of the interpretive process. By the same token, interpreters are being challenged to take responsibility for the theological, social, and ethical implications of their readings.

Biblical interpretation is changing on the practical as well as the theoretical level. More readers, both inside and outside the academic guild, are discovering that the Bible in literary perspective can powerfully engage people's lives. Communities of faith where the Bible is foundational may find that literary criticism can make the Scripture accessible in a way that historical criticism seems unable to do.

Within these changes lie exciting opportunities for all who seek contemporary meaning in the ancient texts. The goal of the series is to encourage such change and such search, to breach the confines of traditional biblical criticism, and to open channels for new currents of interpretation.

—THE EDITORS

FIRE AND ICE

Some say the world will end in fire,
Some say in ice.
From what I've tasted of desire
I hold with those who favor fire.
But if it had to perish twice,
I think I know enough of hate
To say that for destruction ice
Is also great
And would suffice.

— Robert Frost

PREFACE

My first encounter with the Apocalypse was visual—a drama performed on a stage, complete with a narrator, a Greek chorus, changing scenery, and great intensity. The vision was marvelous; nevertheless, I quickly went into the study of social ethics. But on my way back to biblical studies I continued to be intrigued by this often weird and grotesque book.

There have been many conversation partners before and during the writing of this book, which began originally as a co-authored project with Michael Harris. Although Michael was unable to remain involved, the initial discourse began with him ten years ago, when we were both graduate students working on the Apocalypse. Through our endless debates I grew to appreciate even more the necessity of interdisciplinary research. James Blevins was our supervisor (and the director of the above mentioned drama), and his creative pedagogy continues to inspire me.

Much of this book is appearing in other forms and forums. The theses here began in two SBL settings—the Apocalypse consultation and seminar (thanks to David Barr) and the Ideological Criticism consultation and group—and in one fantasy setting, the International Conference of the Fantastic in the Arts. Elisabeth Schüssler Fiorenza has been both encouraging and engaging from the time of my dissertation. I am especially grateful to George Aichele for his knowledge of and passion for the fantastic, but also for his steady responses and support. George and I are part of a somewhat apocalyptic collective writing group whose members include: Fred Burnett, Elizabeth Castelli, Bob Fowler, David Jobling, Stephen Moore, Gary Phillips, Regina Schwartz, and Wilhelm Wuellner. This group gives me hope as we approach the turn of the century. I think that the really risky and uncertain hermeneutical leaps are best made in the company of those who affirm difference.

11

I also want to thank Danna Nolan Fewell and David Gunn for helping support and reshape this project when the original plans changed. And I am indebted to the students in that first eclectic class on apocalyptic who had the courage to challenge and the voices to empower each other and me: Martha Barfield, Frances Fite, Lana Hawkins, Peggy Lyle, and Christie Shin.

I dedicate this book to my husband, Jerry Gentry. He lives out a passionate commitment to justice in his political activities and through his writing, with much creativity and humor.

— TINA PIPPIN

The Marriage of the Lamb—a "somewhat upper-middle-class Marriage" (van der Meer 1978:319)—is a detail from the fifth of the Brussels Tapestries made between 1540 and 1553 in the workshop of Willem de Pannemaker. On the full tapestry the Whore of Babylon is seated on the waters in the lower left corner, holding up the cup with her left hand. In the right corner she is riding the beast, holding up the cup with her right hand. In the detail shown here the Whore appears only mildly displeased at her burning state. The Bride embraces the Lamb and looks adoringly at him. Note that both the Bride and the Whore wear crowns. The wedding guests are as oblivious as the Bride is to the burning female above their heads.

"And the angel said to me, 'Write this: Blessed are those who are invited to the marriage supper of the Lamb.'"
— Apocalypse 19:9

"The body of the silenced woman becomes the main narrative object and locus of meaning, opposite the phallic synecdoche which refers to the male subject and his active inscription of woman's body."
— Lucienne Frappier-Mazur

1

INTRODUCTION: DESIRING APOCALYPSE

Apocalypse and indigestion are given the same edge.
— George Steiner, *Real Presences*

The Apocalypse of John puts the reader in a mood, or rather, in mood swings. In the ecstasy of the visions the reader is commanded to Look! Repent! Conquer! Wake up! Listen! Worship! Rejoice! Come out! Come in! All this action creates a liminal experience for the reader, pushing the reader to the edge, to the end of the world. Here at this edge, this end, is death and desire.

The Apocalypse takes the reader through the visions of John of Patmos. John gives testimony to the seven churches of Asia to the coming chaos and to the final redemption of those who repent and believe the testimony. Jesus appears as a larger-than-life Son of Man and Lamb, who lives and reigns forever in the throne room of God. The twenty-four elders (each in a throne) and the four living creatures surround the throne of God, and they sing hymns of praise to God. Then the destruction is outlined: seven seals are opened, six trumpets are sounded, and seven plagues are set forth. The enemies are destroyed by the army of God, but the true believers are sealed by God and are able to enter the heavenly city. This city is described in great detail, and its wealth and beauty are overwhelming. The narrative ends with the repeated call to heed the prophecy and await the imminent coming of Jesus. Death comes to those who desire the wealth and power of earthly kingdoms; eternal life comes to those who desire the way of the Lamb and the city of God.

In what ways does the reader[1] desire apocalypse? How is desire for complete destruction and partial re-creation enacted and performed by the reader? How are desire and death connected? In this book I will explore this connection, which is ultimately a dis-connection, by reading for the rhetoric of gender (as both social and semiotic construction) in the Apocalypse. Just as there are many forms of death in the Apocalypse, there are many forms of desire. The focus here is on the desire for and death of the female.

If meanings are contingent upon the hermeneutical conventions that the reader brings to the text, then meanings are bound by those sets of conventions. Readers of the Apocalypse are peculiarly bound—bound by a millenarian consciousness and the impact of popular culture influencing interpretation of the book. In this introduction, I want to reveal my ideological biases in reading the Apocalypse. My reading is based on certain political and ethical presuppositions regarding the Apocalypse. I am not concerned with recovering the historical context or the "original audience." In this way I am challenging the presuppositions of dominant Apocalypse scholarship, since I do not assume that Babylon is Rome or that the beast is the emperor Domitian. I want to play with the polyvalence of the symbols, unanchoring them from any specific historical context.

I realize that many biblical scholars want to revise and reconstruct the Apocalypse to relate it to modern sensibilities, but I want to take a postmodern turn: to read the Apocalypse as apocalypse (the designation the text gives itself), which involves entering into the fictional world as a participatory reader. I want to feel and see and hear and touch my way through the narrative. The blood and violence and genocide and ecocide and war and salvation of the few and vision of God's new world is an experience on the cosmic level. This experience is cathartic, involving the emotional release of anger and grief and guilt and joy in the midst of crisis. Catharsis is the central mode of reader response in the Apocalypse. Entering into the fictional world of the Apocalypse involves facing fear and a whole range of feelings.

CATHARSIS, OR APOCALYPTIC AROUSAL

Catharsis is the purgation of undesirable elements in the poet and in the reader (or audience in drama). Many approaches to the concept of catharsis exist since the introduction of the term by Plato and its use by Aristotle. Catharsis is therapeutic, building upon purgation, according to the Freudian definition. Adnan Abdulla (1985:5-6, 9) challenges this traditional Freudian reading of Aristotle by suggesting that once one has experienced the release of emotions, a sense of peace comes.[2] Abdulla reduces catharsis to two elements: (1) emotional arousal that leads to (2) intellectual understanding (clarification) (1985: 9). Abdulla offers the following definition of catharsis:

> . . . catharsis is an aesthetic response which begins with the audience's identification with the protagonist and leads to emotional arousal of conflicting emotions (e.g. fear and pity). These emotions are resolved by their reconciliation, bringing to the audience a sense of elevated harmony, or peace, or repose, which can be thought of as understanding, whether moral, metaphysical, or psychological. (1985:9)[3]

A question behind the investigation of catharsis is, "Does the cathartic experience heal?" T. J. Scheff answers positively, citing the importance of the *ritual* behind catharsis. He states (1979:118-119) that ritual is "the potentially distanced reenactment of situations of emotional distress that are virtually universal in a given culture. . . . Ritual drama, as in the case of Greek tragedy, is concerned with the universal human distresses: death, injustice, betrayal, exile." The individual and the social dimensions of catharsis are included in the definitions by Abdulla and Scheff, and behind these dimensions is the response of the reader of the text or audience at the tragic drama. The Apocalypse is a ritual reenactment of the drama of Christianity at the end of time.

Kenneth Burke (1966:186-187) offers a further explanation of the ritual nature of catharsis: "Catharsis involves fundamentally purgation by the imitation of victimage."[4] This concept of conflict and victimage is also the base of René Girard's (1977; 1986) definition of catharsis as rooted in a social scapegoating process. Girard incorporates the purgation of undesirable elements on a *social* scale. The text (as a homologue of social/communal dynamics) incorporates the scapegoating process into its plot structure. Adopting the Girardian model of catharsis, catharsis functions at two levels: one, at the level of victimage with texts reflecting and maintaining communal moments of scapegoating (at that level catharsis maintains the balance of the community); two, at the level of mythic texts which preserve the mythic moments of scapegoating and texts which subvert these moments. The recognition of the scapegoating process brings a cathartic awareness of one's need/desire to address the whole problem of victimage.

Catharsis emerges either subconsciously or consciously in the act of scapegoating. The slain lamb mythology utilized in the Apocalypse becomes a place of intense tensions between the two types of catharsis, as defined above by Girard. In bringing in the slain Lamb John is utilizing mimesis in the sense that the early Christian communities were called upon to imitate the death of Jesus (martyrdom). John sees "a Lamb standing as if it had been slaughtered" (5:6), and he then sees "under the altar the souls of those who had been slaughtered for the word of God and for the testimony they had given" (6:9). These souls "are they who have come out of the great ordeal; they have washed their robes and made them white in the blood of the Lamb" (7:14).[5]

John's story is a story of conflicting desires emerging out of the two levels of cathartic identification. The slain Lamb from the Exodus tradition is sacrificial. John takes this tradition into his narrative, and makes the slain Lamb a warrior Lamb, defeating forces of evil, that is, the world. If the believers imitate Jesus, they will leave the evil world and enter into his world. In the letters in Apocalypse 2-3 the believers who "conquer" by enduring, repenting, and confessing will be in God's realm, eating of the tree of life (2:7), taking the manna and the white stone (2:17), ruling over the nations and receiving the morning star (2:26-28), wearing the white robe and being included in the book of life (3:5), becoming a pillar in God's temple (3:12), and sitting on the throne with Jesus and God (3:21). The believers imitate Jesus, and Jesus in turn intercedes and confesses their faith to God. The letters give a glimpse of paradise and what the believers are to desire.

With the publication of *Crisis and Catharsis: The Power of the Apocalypse* (1984), Adela Yarbro Collins ushered in a new interpretive paradigm for the study of the Apocalypse. She analyzed the cathartic effect of the Apocalypse, primarily utilizing Aristotle's notion of catharsis (or a particular understanding of it), albeit with slight modification. She supplemented her understanding of catharsis with sociological theory and psychology. This provocative work is a watershed in Apocalypse criticism.

Yarbro Collins derives her understanding of catharsis from her understanding of the social (and psychological) situation of the communities. The communities are suffering from a "perceived crisis" of oppression under Roman imperialism in the late first century CE. Her reading of the social and political situation that is background for the cathartic effect on the reader is indispensable. She has opened up an important and necessary area for study of the Apocalypse.

Drawing on Yarbro Collins, I will examine the emotive dimension of the Apocalypse. The "real" is not excluded from the fictive world of the text. The reader identifies both with the heroes of the narrative and with the fantastic representation of the social order. The function of the political unconscious in the Apocalypse is therapeutic. What was repressed out of fear was shaken, at least while reading or hearing the narrative.

John Gager (1975:51) emphasizes that the Apocalypse is therapy, like psychoanalysis, "whose ultimate goal is to transcend the time between a real present and a mythical future . . . the therapeutic value of myth and psychoanalysis lies in their unique ability to manipulate symbols and in so doing to change reality." He further notes (1975:54) a "rhythmic oscillation" in the narrative between victory/hope (4:1-5:14; 7:1-8:4; 10:1-11:1; 11:15-19; 14:1-7; 15:2-8; 19:1-16; 21:1-22:5) and oppression/despair (6:1-17; 8:5-9:21; 11:2-14; 12:1-17; 13:1-18; 14:8-15:1; 16:1-20; 17:1-18:24; 19:17-20:15). The relationship between the two is dynamic. The myth has freeing power as well as staying power. Time is suppressed (Levi-Strauss), and the reality of oppression is temporarily suspended. The daily drudgery of work (whether slave or free) and the constant presence of dominant powers (whether political or economic) is recalled and then inverted. The Apocalypse is the literary equivalent to a book burning or a food riot or a violent revolutionary takeover. The rhetoric of the Apocalypse intends both a "real" crisis in the "real" world and its solution in the fictive world.

Neither the real nor the fictive is more authentic. However, the attempt (by deconstructionists) to break the relationship between the signifier and the signified has put the signified in "a position outside the sign, where it merges with the referent" (Frow 1986:7-8).[6] No direct referent exists.

Still, the uncertain relation between the signified and signifier produces a powerful discourse. On the level of the symbolic there is a "register shift," as M. A. K. Halliday puts it, in which the oppressed gain the authority and power. The effects of the register (or genre) shift are "that individuals deprived of social power are able to subvert official modes of authority on the symbolic level" or by "a loss of control by agents over the positions they occupy" (Frow 1986:74).[7] In Apocalypse 12 and 13 the reader already knows that the dragon and the beasts do not stand a chance against the Lamb. Heaven is already rejoicing (12:12), even while earth is being deceived. Still, the believers know that they are already in the Lamb's book of life and have nothing to fear. Those who participate in the imperial cult practices are in for a surprise:

> Then another angel, a third, followed them, crying with a loud voice, "Those who worship the beast and its image, and receive a mark on their foreheads or on their hands, they will also drink the wine of God's wrath, poured unmixed into the cup of his anger, and they will be tormented with fire and sulfur in the presence of the holy angels and in the presence of the Lamb. And the smoke of their torment goes up forever and ever. There is no rest day or night for those who worship

20

the beast and its image and for anyone who receives the mark
of its name." (14:9-11)

The prophecy of burning alive forever is strong incentive to
isolate oneself.

The embodiment of evil is found in the symbols of the
Whore and the beasts. In Lacanian terms the beast is a "material signifier" (like the phallus; see Jameson 1981:45). The beast
is an exaggerated symbol for power relations. Domination is in
the forefront, and it is a grotesque monster. All the grandeur is
gone.

Catharsis emerges from the ideas of death and desire from
both within the text and from the critics. These two concepts are
in fact basic, for fear and resentment derive from the inevi-
tability of death and the dynamics of desire. I begin my discussion of death and desire by examining ideology critique and by
raising the problems of catharsis when one reads for gender. As
will be shown, there are also problems with a liberation reading
of the text, for what is liberating for one of the "oppressed" is
not necessarily liberating for all of them.

THE RHETORIC OF DEATH AND DESIRE

Is the Apocalypse a desirable ending to Christian sacred scripture? This is a primary issue to be addressed in this book. The
introduction to the Apocalypse in the New Oxford Annotated
Bible (NRSV, 1991) certainly shows this persuasion:

> The Book of Revelation, or Apocalypse, *is a fitting close to the*
> *Scriptures of the Old and New Testaments,* for its final chap-
> ters depict the consummation toward which the whole biblical
> message of redemption is focused. It may be described as an
> inspired picture-book that, by an accumulation of magnificent
> poetic imagery, makes a powerful appeal to the reader's
> imagination. (364, NT; emphasis mine)

Certainly, a "hermeneutic of acceptance" would deem the
Apocalypse a "fitting close." And certainly, the rhetorical devices
in the Apocalypse itself ideally push the reader to this conclusion.

But desire for the end is complex; a multiplicity of desires is
at work in the Apocalypse, expressed both as desire for desire

(life) and desire for death. Desire and death are linked in the Apocalypse, similar to Derrida's "life death."[8] Thanatos and eros fill the reader's imagination.

Desire in literature is defined in many ways and linked not only with death but also with truth, reason, or ideology.[9] The basic move is from Freudian preoccupation with desire as sexual to a broadening of the definition to include, according to Sam Girgus, "a wish for love, completion and recognition" (1990:5). Girgus further defines desire as "the seething chaos of inarticulate wishes" (1990:7), while making an important connection between ideology and eros. Girgus's definition is especially fitting for the Apocalypse, where chaos precedes order and crowds the narrative space.

The connections made by Georges Bataille (1986:11) are also helpful: "Eroticism, it may be said, is assenting to life up to the point of death . . . there does remain a connection between death and sexual excitement."[10] I want to expose the tension between death and desire in the Apocalypse and explore the effect of this tension on the reader. Catharsis as an emotional arousal leads to intellectual clarity in ritual. The various emotions that are aroused in the reader are centered around the rhetoric of death and desire, the concept of martyrdom and hope in God's utopian world. Thus, desire is not defined as a lack, but as a powerful tool of social change.

What to do with death—the social taboo of death by the imperial power and the public exposing of the dead body (Jezebel and her followers, the two witnesses, the Whore, the flesh of the mighty)—is a central concern in the text. What to do with desire—the desire for power and wealth as symbolized in the body of the Whore and the desire for God's world as symbolized in the body of the Bride—is another central concern. The rhetoric of the text moves, pushes, even terrorizes the reader to make a choice between the Lamb and the Beast. The deaths of the Lamb (and his followers) and of the Beast (and his monstrous cohorts) frame the narrative. Choose the Lamb and death becomes eternal life; choose the Beast and death is eternal death.

OUTLINE OF THE BOOK

This book moves from more general ideological/political readings to an incorporation of Marxist-feminist readings, using the
discourse with studies in the fantastic as central. The multiple
voices from different scholarly disciplines will hopefully show a
range of possibilities for Apocalypse studies. Some readings
place the Apocalypse in a more positive light than others; an
easy criticism is that my particular reading begins more positively than it ends. I do not see positive and negative readings as
oppositional; rather, the Apocalypse is an oppositional text in
itself. The art of the female figures in the Apocalypse shows the
gender oppositions. I have incorporated representative art from
the medieval period to the twentieth century to provide a visual
lens for reading for gender.

In chapter 2 the issue of method in reading for the themes
of death and desire will be explored. Ideology critique will
provide the methodological bridge between the narratological
and hermeneutical approaches. Political poetics involves the
conversation between the textual signs and levels on the one
hand, and the unconscious ideology and class concerns of the
text on the other ("narrative as a socially symbolic act," in the
words of Fredric Jameson). The Apocalypse as fantasy literature
will be introduced in this chapter.

Chapter 3 will be a basic introduction to the questions
raised by a feminist biblical hermeneutic. I want to push against
the boundaries (visible and invisible) in Apocalypse studies by
including the multiple discourse between biblical studies and
feminist and political criticism. The issues raised by reading for
gender and the female characters will be introduced in this
chapter.

Chapters 4 and 5 will explore the "sexual/textual politics"
(Toril Moi) of the narrative, using studies in gender and reading
as the main interpretive strategy. Reading the text as a woman
demands reading for the gender codes in the narrative where
women appear or are noticeably absent. The archetypes of
women (virgin and whore) show the displacement of women in
the text. This "gynocritical" approach will expose the patriarchal systems of the text and reflect the authority of feminist

readings. The effects of reading as a woman will be the central focus of these chapters, which will lead further into the discussion of death and desire.

The concluding chapter will utilize contemporary deconstructive theory in order to discuss the narrative tensions in the text (or what Barbara Johnson calls "warring forces of signification"). I will not "destruct" the Apocalypse but show how and where the text is in tension and conflict with itself. This mode of analysis will lead to a discussion of the theological implications of the analysis of death and desire done throughout the book. As I push against the boundaries of interpretation, I intend for my own reading to be pushed and challenged, opening the way to more interpretive moves, or rather, more visions of the future.

2

THE POLITICS
OF THE END
OF THE WORLD:
METHOD
AND
MADNESS

As we approach the year 2000 and become more and more aware of the millenarian consciousness that certain religious groups make central, the response of biblical scholars in the academy to the more literal renderings of the text is increasingly important. Important avenues for response are opening, moreover, as the discourses of sociology, cultural anthropology, and literary theory are being incorporated by Apocalypse scholars.

I want to push against the old boundaries of interpreting genre/form and take the text as a whole with all its movements and gaps and times and spaces. Multiple readings of the Apocalypse are possible and indeed necessary.[1] I offer only one of many possible readings of the Apocalypse—only one possible way to push the boundaries of reading.

Apocalypse as a genre has always been a slippery term, despite the enormous effort put into compiling all the accompanying laundry lists of elements; no "apocalypse" ever has all the elements. A form critical approach sees the text in terms of fragments and pieces of a whole puzzle. Or rather, it looks at the whole in order to search for the pieces, and then returns to the whole.

The term "literary devices" is often too loosely used by biblical scholars. A "device" is "an artistic contrivance in a literary work used to achieve a particular effect" (*The American Heritage Dictionary*). Examples of literary devices include irony, characterization, and focalization. These devices, however, must not be confused with the form(s) that structure the text as a whole.

Further, form critical categories and narratological terms need to be kept separate. Form criticism is interested in the *Sitz im Leben* and the so-called historical context, which newer forms of literary theory are not concerned with (in particular, reader-response theory, poststructuralism and deconstruction). New Testament scholars are tempted to use literary theory in order to find another way of reaching the so-called historical context of the text. For example, in reader-response theory the implied reader is often mistaken as synonymous with the original audience. The search for the so-called historical context of the Apocalypse takes many forms, all of which cannot be described here. I am arguing against coopting literary theory and sociological constructs to reconstruct the "real" first century environment of the text.

I understand that Apocalypse scholars are in the difficult spot of dealing with contemporary historical misappropriations of this text, and these readings present a hermeneutical and ethical challenge. The poststructural critique presents a challenge to all biblical scholars: ultimately we are left with the text; all we have is the text. In the end, all we have is what the text tells us. Or in the words of Patrocinio Schweickart (1986:47), "In reading, one encounters only a text, the trail of an absent author." When we speak of "context," we speak vaguely. And we speak of a space with an absent author.

The emphasis in Apocalypse scholarship has been on finding the inner cohesion of the Apocalypse and how everything fits together. The search is for order, and this search is conducted on the surface level of the text. Literary theory urges us deeper, into the deep structures of the text, into its rhetoric, into its infinite multiple voices.

A literary-critical reading of the Apocalypse is not set in

terms of history and recovery of the "original audience." The text can be understood in terms of mixed genre. As Fredric Jameson (1975:142) makes clear, genres are not to be seen "in terms of fixed form." Ultimately, I refer to the Apocalypse as "apocalypse" out of convenience and deference to the Greek title. I want to suggest, nonetheless, that we shift the way we talk about the form of the Apocalypse to allow for textual gaps which produce an open, unstable text (Bakhtin's polyphonic novel, for example, or Barthes' "plural text" or "open poetics").[2]

Contemporary literary theory calls for a shift from concerns for author/history/form to attention to the role of the reader and reading conventions. To return to the original reading/readers is impossible. Peter Rabinowitz (1987:26; following Northrop Frye) points away from a "pure reading" to the conventions in the play between signifier and signified: "Rather, you need to ask what sort of *corrupted* reader this particular author wrote for: what were that reader's beliefs, engagements, commitments, prejudices, and stampedings of pity and terror?" Instead of making everything fit smoothly into an apocalyptic form, reader-oriented theory allows room for the emotive and the cathartic experience of the reader—both the implied and contemporary reader.

Since readers come to the text with presuppositions and sacks of specific methodological tools, in this chapter I want to outline my method of reading. The starting point is a literary reading that focuses on the political and ethical dimensions of the text, known as ideology critique. Ideology critique examines the interaction between text and reader and scrutinizes the interpretive moves the reader makes. Ideology critique is based on the idea that texts are produced (and continue to be produced) in political "contexts." In other words, texts that are given authority in a community affect people's lives. I am interested in the ways the Apocalypse influences women's (and men's) lives. I will trace the move from ideology critique to political readings of the fantastic, a subversive literature of the supernatural.

ENVISIONING DESIRE: WHO IS WORTHY?

Then another angel, a second, followed, saying, "Fallen, fallen is Babylon the great! She has made all nations drink of the wine of the wrath of her fornication."

This proclamation from Apocalypse 14:8 reveals the intensity of the political relations. The cathartic experience of the reader at the death of the Whore is the ultimate release of a colonized people. The ruling power is symbolized in the female body and is destroyed in a great ritual of murder.

Apocalyptic literature is an outlet of responding to political repression. The Apocalypse of John is an example of the spirit of discontent and the split with dominant ideology. The goal and hope is the fall of Babylon. The struggle here (contra Marx, who thought that most class struggles were latent) is open, and the language (contra some apocalypse scholars, who say apocalyptic language is hidden in mysterious code) is open. The symbolic language is attainable by both oppressed and oppressors. Herein lies the danger, the danger that some early Christians (the martyrs) did not avoid but that Christianity with Constantine averted.

The political agenda of the Apocalypse is revolution; God and company fight the evil power and win and set up a new heavenly city for the followers of the Lamb. The pyramid is upended and social structures radically reversed (the oppressors and all who support them are destroyed!). The status quo is violently opposed by the heavenly forces. The earthly "forces" are to take sides and resist the "seduction" of Babylon: "Come out of her my people, so that you do not take part in her sins, and so that you do not share in her plagues" (18:4).

One way to consider the Apocalypse is as "resistance literature."[3] The believers are called to resist temptations and falsities: "But I have this against you: you tolerate that woman Jezebel, who calls herself a prophet and is teaching and beguiling my servants to practice fornication and to eat food sacrificed to idols" (2:20). Those who do not repent "of their murders or their sorceries or their fornication or their thefts" (9:21) will be destroyed. But those who resist "will inherit these things, and I will be their God and they will be my children" (21:7). They can enter into the heavenly city (22:14), while "outside are the dogs and sorcerers and fornicators and murderers and idolaters and everyone who loves and practices falsehood" (22:15). The vivid discrepancies between insider and outsider urge the reader to resist the powers of evil: the Nicolaitans, Balaam, Jezebel, Babylon, Satan (the dragon/serpent), and the beasts.

Conflict is central; those who enter the utopian city have resisted the previously dominant powers. The prevailing "realism" which determined the societal structure said, basically, "This is the way things are." This "realism" is split and disrupted in the Apocalypse through a fracturing of the signifier and the signified (fracturing the sign). In other words the chain of signification is broken (Coward/Ellis 1977:67).[4] This process of signification involves the language process and is *not* to be confused with the social process. The Apocalypse says, "For in one hour all this wealth has been laid waste" (18:17 and 19).

Fredric Jameson explains the relationship between history and text in his "negative dialectic." Jameson (1981:35) proposes:

> . . . that history is *not* a text, not a narrative, master or other-wise, but that, as an absent cause, it is inaccessible to us except in textual form, and that our approach to it and to the Real itself necessarily passes through its prior textualization, its narrativization in the political unconscious.[5]

History both is and is not a narrative. The orneriness of dialectical thinking is characteristic of Jameson's arguments. On the level of the superstructure (culture, ideology, and politics) the components share identity and difference, but the identity is in the background. In the frustration inherent in attempting to follow dialectical argumentation the questions are raised: Is a Marxist literary theory talking about real historical development or not? Is History a narrative or not? Jameson's answer is, predictably, that History is both. And so the dialectical circle continues.

In keeping with the dialectic of imagination, history is and is not part of ideology, whether one calls history "absent cause" (Jameson) or the "double absence" (Eagleton 1976:62). Pierre

Macherey (1978:60) speaks to this concept in his famous statement: "We always eventually find, at the edge of the text, the
language of ideology, momentarily hidden, but eloquent by its
very absence."[6] Roland Barthes (1986:138) echoes this idea
when he states that "historical discourse is essentially an ideological elaboration or, to be more specific, an *imaginary* elaboration." Thus, ideology involves both social relations and
linguistic constructs.

A central question is how does all this criticism relate to
biblical studies and in particular to the Apocalypse of John? On
a basic level, although everything I really need to know about
the political "context" of the Apocalypse is in the text itself, the
class struggle of the first century provides the base (or motor) of
interpretation. Ideology critique cuts into the text, undercutting
the prevailing bourgeois interpretations. An ideological rereading of the Apocalypse is liberating because it brings to the
surface the traces of alienation and fear and oppression. In
other words, ideology critique brings to the surface the unconscious of the text, but this reading also raises many problems in
interpretation. What may be one person's utopia may be another's dystopia. First, I will trace the more positive, liberating
reading of the Apocalypse which is based on the class struggle
and the hopes of the underclasses. Then I will show the problems in a generalized liberation reading. If the Apocalypse offers
hope, what is the shape of this hope?

THE MARX ON THE FOREHEAD:
POLITICIZING DEATH AND DESIRE

Pure literature does not exist; all literature is political. This
strong assumption is basic for Terry Eagleton in his political
criticism. The consciousness of the dominant class, of those who
own and control the economic and political systems, is false.
And when the political ideology of a text is tapped, literature
has a transformative function; literature makes the reader a
"better person" (Eagleton 1983:208). Eagleton continues: "It
must be a question of political and not only of "moral" argument . . . it must be *genuine* moral argument, which sees the
relations between individual qualities and values and our whole

material conditions of existence." The politics of the interpretative process are always there.

Jameson, who focuses on history in terms of the struggle between oppressed and oppressor, calls for a political reading of history that uncovers the political unconscious which has been repressed. Jameson's plan involves "detecting the traces of that uninterrupted narrative, in restoring to the surface of the text the repressed and buried reality of this fundamental history, that the doctrine of a political unconscious finds its function and its necessity" (Jameson 1981:20).[7] The oppressed repress their struggle in order to survive in an unjust world.[8] The oppressed thus experience alienation and anomie. Related is Nietzsche's concept of *ressentiment* in which the weak desire suffering and oppression. Denial is easier than acceptance, as the letters in Apocalypse 2-3 show.

The angels of the seven churches are each given a message from "him who holds the seven stars in his right hand, who walks among the seven golden lampstands" (2:1) and of "the first and the last, who was dead and came to life" (2:8) and "who has the sharp two-edged sword" (2:12) and "the Son of God, who has eyes like a flame of fire, and whose feet are like burnished bronze" (2:18) and "who has the seven spirits of God and the seven stars" (3:1) and "the holy one, the true one, who has the key of David" (3:7) and "the Amen, the faithful and true witness, the origin of God's creation" (3:14). The repetition of the description of the speaker from 1:12-16 emphasizes his authority. The churches are given the opportunity to hear and repent and conquer. There is great hope for those who endure oppression and resist alternatives other than God.

Jameson realizes that calling forth the painful reality of oppression is difficult. Often feelings of alienation and detachment are increased. So, in order to survive the oppressed develop "strategies of containment" in which to mask their unconscious. Literature is one such strategy. The structuralist theory of Greimas is helpful here. In Greimas's semiotic square, which represents the "totality" of history (and lived experience), structures of reality are set forth. Where there are textual gaps, or parts of the text that do not fit into the square, there lies the repressed unconscious. The task of ideology critique is to seek out those semiotic gaps and dig into those deep structures. Greimas is operating at the actantial (roles) level and Jameson at the political level. Greimas is concerned with sentence structure and Jameson with social structure.[9] Negative dialectics is at work in finding the cause in the absent cause. In other words, what the text does *not* say is as (or more) important than what the text *does* say.

The political critic is somewhat like a detective, sleuthing around likely corners as well as the unlikely, often unnoticed places of the text. And like a detective, the political critic often goes by "hunches." At least there is one "hunch," namely that history is grounded in the class struggle (i.e., History). For Jameson any interpretation that represses History is unacceptable.

The traditional biblical exegete will probably bristle at any interpretation that hints at or includes an allegorical reading of the biblical text. Jameson is not interested in these historical-critical logistics; instead, he seeks to place priority on the ideology of the reading process as it affects the individual and more importantly the totality of human relationships. In the medieval example Jameson raises the ideological investment of medieval Christians (i.e., to interpret Hebrew Scriptures through the lens of Jesus Christ) to the surface and shows how their reading operated as a dialectic.[10] There is more at stake in all this than the thesis that interpretation is subjective. The point is to see the relationship between History and narrative and how these relate to the individual and the social totality. If narrative is "a socially symbolic act," then the historical story is understood in terms of ideologies, repressed emotions, and collective praxis. Jameson focuses on the History that generates the narrative and not on the reader.

Narrative is seen as a form in which the class struggle is known, or can be known. As the political unconscious is brought to the textual surface, so is the reader's own repressed unconscious made conscious. When the reader is not in touch with the unconscious, alienation is the result.

Jameson borrows the concept of "horizon" from Hans-Georg Gadamer (1975) to show the range of his theory of interpretation in terms of history and epistemology. The rereading and rewriting of a text moves from narrow to wider concerns, or horizons: from political history, to the social order, and then to an understanding of history (past, present, and future) based on modes of production and commodity fetish.[11] In other words, a text is analyzed by its historical subtext, the *ideologeme* ("the smaller intelligible unit of the essentially antagonistic collective discourse of social classes"), and the "ideology of form" (the symbolic language representing modes of production) (Jameson:1981:76, 81). Each of these semantic horizons is immanently formed and based in History and the class struggle. The starting point is the text (or more specifically, the subtext of the political history of a text).

Jameson is involved in deconstruction by rewriting narrative. A negative dialectic is at work in which History is and is not a narrative. So when the subtext is uncovered and the political kernel is found, what is really found is and is not the context of the narrative. Perhaps "context" is better written and understood in quotes, because in Jameson's hermeneutical enterprise the "context" is symbolic. The social, political, and economic relationships are certainly "real," but in a Marxist format the historical "context" necessarily pushes toward the next horizon. The "context" is known, therefore, only through the political rereading of a text.

The focus on the modes of production introduces a new problem, that of absolutizing the Marxist act of interpretation. Jameson states that the political reading is "the absolute horizon of all reading and all interpretation" (Jameson 1981:17). For Marxism the story of History is the "single great collective story," presented in a symbolic form that needs to be deconstructed and reconstructed.

Transcendent interpretation is defined by Jameson not only in terms of what non-Marxists do. Some of the formalists do it; the New Critics do it; some of the Derridians do it; and doing it means a depoliticizing of the text. I would like to add here that the Christian fundamentalists outdo all the others in doing it (especially with the Apocalypse of John). Transcendent interpretation detaches the text from its historical "context." According to Raman Selden (1985:48), "Transcendent interpretation tries to master the text and in so doing *impoverishes* its true complexity." Does the transcendent interpretation sound a little like an allegorical reading of the text? The immediate answer is yes, but Jameson has a more positive view of allegory. When a text is reread using a master code, or what is also called a "transcendental signified," interpretation occurs on the allegorical level. The transcendental interpretation (using the example of the New Critics) is made "to blurt out its master code and thereby reveal its metaphysical and ideological underpinnings" (Jameson 1981:21-22; cf. 58-59).[12] The movement to the ethical and spiritual levels allows for a total immanent rereading of the text. Once the interpreter is up front about the ideology, the distance from the text is shortened.

Immanently apparent in this interpretation are the contradictions of the text. Contradictions occur in social relations between classes. These contradictions are repressed in the political unconscious. The narrative provides solutions for the major contradictions in its unconscious (Jameson 1981:79-82). Contradiction implies paradox (antinomy) and anxiety (aporia). The transcendent interpretation is far removed from the textual contradictions and thereby misses the point of the text's political reality. By standing outside the text, the transcendent readers are merely promoting their own ideology about the end of the world, and are not paying close attention to the vision of the text.

Greimas's semiotic square is helpful in locating contradiction in a text, because the square is based on the relationship of binary opposition. In revealing the binary oppositions the semiotic square also reveals the repressed political unconscious. The textual apparatus of plot, characters, signs and symbols interact beneath the surface in contradiction and opposition. For example, in the Apocalypse of John there is the discourse between good and evil. The political reading of these symbols is basically concerned not with smoothing over the paradoxes of the Woman Clothed with the Sun in chapter 12 and the Whore in chapter 14, but with raising the political, social, and economic issues that are represented by these women. There is a definite class struggle in the Apocalypse that the transcendental readings have rendered non-existent in terms of its historical "context." The binary oppositions are important for Jameson's immanent Marxist interpretation of literature because they point to the struggle between oppressed and oppressor, haves and have-nots.

Related to the contradictions inherent in the text are what Jameson calls the politicized notions of desire and freedom. These Freudian notions are part of the text's deep structure. Cornel West (1983:181) explains the politicized notion of desire as promising "access to a revolutionary energy lurking beneath the social veil of appearances, an energy capable of negating the reified present order."[13] This notion of desire expresses the energy of the subtext and the energy of the latent class struggle (for Marx). In other words, the notions of desire and freedom are latent in the political unconscious of the text, and are the forces behind hope and praxis (West 1983:180). The concept of freedom is at work in repressed times and is for Jameson "the privileged instrument of a political hermeneutic" (Jameson 1971:84).[14] Freedom from oppression is what the oppressed desire, and this desire always exists, albeit mostly hidden by the dominant ideology. Thus, desire is linked "directly and without mediation to power and resistance" (Grosz 1989:xvi).

In apocalyptic literature this desire for freedom is not latent but clearly out in the open. God's army conquers the evil powers, and a paradise is set up for the believers. Jameson would say that only a political hermeneutic is the proper interpretive tool to use when reading apocalyptic. Binary oppositions are not ignored in a political reading of the text; rather, they offer hope in their final "solution" and encourage praxis. One is either in the book of life or not; if not, then the lake of fire is the place reserved for political enemies (20:15).

Jameson leads us to a view of the totality of a narrative in its historical "context." Jameson's intent is to fashion the future by transforming the mode of production. The latent is made open, and the not-said is said. Does this process sound idealistic? Of course. A future vision of the transformation is in mind. But in Jameson's terms this vision is utopian. A dialectic is at work between ideology and utopia. Capitalism has produced contradictions in the division of labor and control of the modes of production. The utopian vision is part of the feelings of alienation and paternalism that accompany the capitalist system. The utopian vision is present in dehumanizing situations. Jameson attributes this need for utopianism to the destructive structure of capitalism, and claims that modernism expresses the ideology of capitalism and a "utopian compensation" for repressed reality (Jameson 1981:42, 236-237). Meanwhile the negative dialectic of Marxism is at work in the dialectic of utopia and ideology, bringing to light the tension between the dominant and the dominated. Jameson sounds this note of liberation:

> Ideological commitment is not first and foremost a matter of moral choice but of the taking of sides in a struggle between fragmented social life . . . the political thrust of the struggle of all groups against each other can never be immediately universal but must always necessarily be focused on the class enemy. (Jameson 1981:290)

The utopian vision is not some universal story of the world turned upside down. Rather, the vision is based on a particular history and political existence of a specific people. The reader takes ideological sides. The reader is either identified with the oppressed or with the oppressor.

A theological response to the notion of utopia is given by Reinhold Niebuhr. Niebuhr would probably appreciate Jameson's work because it is not grounded in either philosophy or science, but in politics. Jameson is more up front about what Niebuhr calls Marxism's "apocalyptic vision" (1932:155). Bringing religion into the political scene, Niebuhr states:

> Wherever religion concerns itself with the problems of society, it always gives birth to some kind of millennial hope, from the perspective of which present social realities are convicted of inadequacy, and courage is maintained to continue in the effort to redeem society of injustice. The courage is needed; for the task of building a just society seems always a hopeless

one when only present realities and immediate possibilities are envisaged. (Niebuhr, 1932:61)

The utopian vision is not some idealistic trance that requires distance from political reality. Rather, the utopian vision is the motor of the notion of desire and freedom, and the final wish-fulfillment of the oppressed. The reality of hunger, political oppression, and economic deprivation drives humanity to the brink of History, and there is found the desire for the transformation of the world.

More than most Marxists, Jameson is amenable to theological concerns, and his literary theory provides the base which is greatly needed in liberation theology and liberation hermeneutics. To read from below means first of all to know how to read—how to read textual signs in order to dig up the political unconscious. The political method of reading from Jameson and Eagleton is directed to the educated elite, and it can be understandably argued that these highly complex literary theories make little, if any, difference to the poor of the world. But the point here is that the application of these narrative theories is important on more than the theoretical level. Jameson's project is positive and headed toward an end (contra Althusser) where collective praxis is the norm.

There is an ethical push and pull in ideological criticism that is dialectical on the theory level and practical on the social level. The incredible tension of the not yet and the not said pushes and pulls the reader who is not doing. Still, the intellectual activity of literary theory can never be directly beneficial to those in the third world. An ideological critical reading does have as an underpinning the desire for the transformation of the world, and is transforming at least one small segment of oppressors!

Furthermore, since the oppressed communicate to the world through stories (of memory and desire), the skills of listening and interpreting are important for dialogue. The discourse between classes reveals a great deal about the power play of relationships. As far as relationships with texts are concerned, a complimentary concept for Marxist theory is the study of discourse and power. Terry Eagleton (1983:118) is direct about the transforming power of discourse: "[it] achieves something in the saying: it is language as a kind of material practice in itself, discourse as social action."[15] The reader listens in on the textual discourses, and these discourses have a powerful effect in return.

What is going on at the level of discourse and power? First of all, the conversation is political, as Eagleton and Jameson make clear. Secondly, according to John Frow (1986), power invests discourse with the ideology of the dominant class. Thirdly, resistance is a necessary part of discourse. Frow introduces an interesting aspect of the speech act:

> Utterance is in principle dialogic. Both ideology and resistance are *uses* of discourse, and both are "within" power . . . Resistance is the possibility of fracturing the ideological from within or of turning it against itself (as in children's language games) or of reappropriating it for counterhegemonic purposes. (1986:63-64)

When the oppressed can no longer accept discourse on the terms of the oppressors, resistance is employed. The language game becomes a subversive act, and apocalyptic literature is an open example of the literary form of resistance to the dominant ideology. Resistance literature is a discourse formed by power— the power that the powerless can wield to reverse the dominant ideology.

Derrida (1982:89) notes, "Nothing is less conservative than the apocalyptic genre." These words point to the essentially disruptive function of apocalyptic literature. Apocalyptic literature is dangerous territory, because it is in itself deconstructive; the unconscious emotive responses to oppression are on the surface and are acted out in the plot by vivid characters. Apocalyptic literature digs up repressed feelings and urges the reader to participate in the cathartic act.

Binary oppositions in the text reveal the historical class struggle and the dialectical tension between powerlessness and the desire to overcome this status. The Apocalypse of John is unified through its plot and characters and narrator, to be sure, but the text is also wrapped up in ideology. Ideology has its limitations, but the energy of the narrative is nonetheless structured by it. The Apocalypse is certainly an energetic text, often jerking the reader from scene to scene. Its rapid panorama of the world's history, from creation to church struggles to the end and transformation of creation, engenders the appropriate response, "Amen. Come, Lord Jesus!" (22:20).

SUBVERSIVE IMAGINATION: FANTASY AND DISASTER

Beginnings and endings are times of anxiety and crisis as well as of possibility and transformation. In speaking of his hope for the totality of society, Ernst Bloch commented that "the true genesis is not at the beginning, but at the end" (Bloch 1971: 44).[16]

The Apocalypse of John focuses on the end and creates a space for these anxieties and hopes to roam freely. Just as Bloch is forthright about the goal of history as the transformation of the world, so is the Apocalypse involved in a similar teleological drive. This incredible apocalyptic journey, complete with beasts and angels, gods and demons, dragon and lamb, a queen and a whore, and a cast of thousands (of both good and evil people), takes the reader to the edge—the edge of history and materialism and faith and desire and, finally, the infinite edge of the imagination. The Apocalypse is a writing of the final revolution, where God is in command and the transformation of the natural and social orders is complete.

To borrow from Maurice Blanchot (1986:1), the Apocalypse is "the writing of the disaster": "The disaster ruins everything, all the while leaving everything intact . . . the infiniteness of the threat has in some way broken every limit." The disaster is always there—just under the surface—and once we've heard about it, no amount of "psychic numbing" can block it out entirely. The Apocalypse makes the disaster imminent, conscious, while calling the reader into responsibility for its presence/nonpresence. The Apocalypse writes of the disaster, and the reading of the disaster changes everything while at the same time leaving change as a possibility—a threat.

I explore what I see as the desire and truth of this "writing of the disaster" through a study of what Jameson (1981) calls "the dialectic of utopia and ideology." I read the Apocalypse as a dialectic between the utopian desire for global transformation and the truth of the ideologies. The hermeneutic which has been developed thus far will be nuanced here by a discussion of theories of textual ideology and literary production in conversation with studies in the fantastic genre. As we have seen already, the dialogue of biblical studies with ideology critique creates revolutionary ways of textual interpretation.

The mode of apocalyptic literature is a discourse with engaging images and action. The repressed political unconscious is central in its fantastic visions. The importance of genre is necessary to acknowledge, because the apocalyptic genre is a marginal one, written by the disenfranchised to express their desire for the future transformation of society. The contradictions of daily life are lived out in the writing, and these contradictions are dramatized in a story of powerful imagination.[17] As the reader joins the imagining, the apocalyptic discourse subverts.

Jameson (1981:106) describes genres as "essentially literary *institutions*, or social contracts between a writer and a specific public, whose function is to specify the proper use of a particular cultural artifact." In examining Ernst Bloch's work on the fairy tale, Jameson finds a significant function of the genre. The fairy tale is "a systematic deconstruction and undermining of the hegemonic aristocratic form of the epic" (1981:86; cf. 1971: 130). In the Apocalypse the heroes of the dominant power (dragon and beasts) are the villains, and the powerless Christians are the victors. The aristocrats not only lose their status; they are destroyed. Like the fairy tales of the Brothers Grimm, the apocalyptic genre turns the status quo into a farce.

The Apocalypse can be compared with children's fairy tales in that both can function to raise social (and political) consciousness. Jack Zipes (1986b:8) discusses the power relations in fairy tales:

> The fact that the people as carriers of tales do not *explicitly* seek a total revolution of social relations does not minimize the utopian aspect in the *imaginative* portrayal of class conflict. Whatever the outcomes of the tales are . . . the impulse

and critique of the "magic" are rooted in an historically explicable desire to overcome oppression and change society.

The power of genre for Jameson lies in the opposition of the Saussurian concepts of *langue* and *parole*. Simply put, *langue* represents language systems and *parole* denotes individual utterances. What is at stake is the individual's relation to the class. The "crucial moment" of the fairy or folk tale is in *langue*, that is, in its collective essence. In other words, the fairy tale has power not in its individualistic roots but in the way it relates to the social structures it opposes and in its collective praxis.

The story of oppression and liberation in the Apocalypse is a fantasy, which Katherine Hume (1984:21) defines as "any departure from consensus reality." The monster beasts are effective symbols for expressing political unconscious which contradicts the status quo. Fantastic literature reaches into that other world where the unconscious is set free.

The Apocalypse is a "mythic fantasy," according to Northrop Frye's classification of myth as a mode of fiction. In terms of the hero (or protagonist) Frye (1957:33) notes: "If superior in *kind* both to other men and to the environment of other men, the hero is a divine being, and the story about him will be a *myth* in the common sense of a story about a god." The reader identifies easily with the hero; in the Apocalypse the identification is with Jesus and John and the forces of good (the angels, the witnesses, and the Woman giving birth). The hero is part of the other world that the reader desires.

This other world is fantastic. Tzvetan Todorov (1975:32-34) outlines three conditions necessary for fantastic literature: the readers must hesitate in their identification with the hero; the readers "hesitate between a natural and a supernatural explanation of the events described," and the readers must reject allegorical and poetic readings of the text. In other words, there is room for doubt and hesitation on the part of the reader, who is caught in the tension between the real and the imaginary. The fantastic is dangerous for the bourgeois interpreter because it subverts the dominant reality, but this genre is also dangerous for the oppressed because it "may evaporate any moment" (Todorov 1975:41). Thus, all readers share this hesitation.

In Todorov's terms (1975:44-52), this hesitation occurs between the fantastic-uncanny and the fantastic-marvelous. The uncanny is when reasonable explanations are given for supernatural acts. No such explanation for the supernatural is given in the fantastic-marvelous. The fantastic discourse in the Apocalypse is marvelous because no rational (only a faith-based) reason for the visions is given at the end and throughout the narrative.[18] The reader is caught between two worlds, the natural and the supernatural, and is constantly made aware of the realities of oppression and hope for liberation. The uncanny marks the dangerous journey for the reader into the supernatural and back home again.

Other definitions of the fantastic abound.[19] Colin Manlove (1982:17) defines fantasy as "a fiction evoking wonder and containing a substantial and irreducible element of supernatural or impossible worlds, beings or objects with which the mortal characters in the story or the readers become on at least partly familiar terms." Manlove (1983:1-14) further states that the difference between modern and traditional fantasy is that traditional fantasy does not explain the details of the story. He includes the Bible in his list of fantasy works. In the Apocalypse the reader is able to participate in someone else's fantasy, which is consciously or unconsciously the reader's own.

The reader of fantastic literature does not escape reality by reading tales of the supernatural. The Apocalypse is not escapist literature. A Marxist interpretation of the fantastic by Rosemary Jackson legitimizes this claim. Jackson (1981:20) expands the work of Todorov and others, proposing the following definition:

> Fantasy re-combines and inverts the real, but it does not escape it: it exists in a parasitical or symbiotic relation to the real. The fantastic cannot exist independently of that "real" world which it seems to find so frustratingly finite.[20]

Tobin Siebers takes a middle position in his study of the Romantic fantastic, pointing to the inseparableness of the supernatural and the "real," social world. Siebers (1984:45) focuses on the superstition factor present in the Romantic fantastic and suggests that this literature "descends into every conceivable kind of violence . . . [and] seems a poor form of escapism, but it may be a means of examining and reinterpreting social formations." Siebers is correct in raising the anthropological issues of superstition and violent desires (using Girard) present in the literature. But he fails to take seriously the subversive nature of the fantastic as raised by the Marxist critics. In fact, Siebers' notions of superstition and violence (Girard's scapegoat mechanism) aid in an understanding of the social reality presented by the text that does not exclude its subversive function. The experience of anarchy and release in the dreams and visions of the fantastic are connected with "real" conflicts; the fantastic is not a flight from reality.

Fantasy affects the reader politically because the relationship between the real and fictive worlds is political. For Jackson (1981:26) fantastic literature attacks the "real" of bourgeois domination in order to subvert the dominant order. Jameson (1981:134) also notes this phenomenon, which he sees beginning at the end of the nineteenth century. There he finds "the place of the fantastic as a determinate, marked *absence* at the heart of the secular world." The negativity and absence is actually positive, since it is based in history and the class struggle. The "real" is what is to be overcome. If this victory is not possible in this natural world, conquest is certainly possible in the supernatural world. Participation is thus possible in the fantastic, not as a way of reentering the "real" with new ways to live. Rather, the Apocalypse as fantasy opens up ethical implications. The Apocalypse story both seduces and changes the reader. For the oppressed the narrative is subversive, but for the oppressor it is perverse. In a postmodern understanding of genre, the ethical is the interpretive key.

3

AN APOCALYPSE
OF WOMEN:
SUBVERTING
CATASTROPHE

In the late twentieth century we are living on the edge of apocalypse. Natural disasters, wars, and new social and cultural movements are interpreted by some as signs and symbols of the end of time. Is the end of this millennium "closing time" (Norman O. Brown) or the beginning of what Rosemary Radford Ruether calls "the radical kingdom"? Is this time before the turn of the century the time when the prophetic scroll is rolled out as the script for the final battle (Apoc 20), as fundamentalist Christians propose? Or is this turn into a new century a postmodern turn—a turn into a mosaic of the wealth of global dreams and visions of the future?

Conflicting readings of these apocalyptic times produce a multiplicity of voices. These voices do not only conflict but compete for control and for acknowledgement as the authoritative voice. The biblical text of the Apocalypse of John is the space of the interpretive battle. The dominant reading of the Apocalypse in popular Christian culture has been a literal one in which all the apocalyptic symbols are made static, and the text is ripped out of its first century CE context. Many fundamentalists actually rewrite the Apocalypse to fit their own conservative political agendas which are based on cold war rhetoric of the Soviet Union as "other" or on any current perceived political threat as "other." Although the second half of the twentieth century has brought more biblical scholars of the academy to the Apocalypse, most of these studies are caught in the slow trickle-down effect. For most mainline churches and biblical scholars, the Apocalypse of John is still at best marginally canonical.

The end of a thousand years brings renewed fervor to studying the Apocalypse, as the last decade of the second thousand years of Christianity shows. The Persian Gulf Crisis in 1990 and 1991 received headlines like, "Armageddon Prophecy: Gulf Crisis May Herald War to End All Wars" and "Is the Gulf Conflict the Last Battle? Theological Forces Clash." Richard Lee of Rehoboth Baptist Church in Atlanta proclaimed Saddam Hussein as the beast of the Apocalypse. And a housewife in Georgia was quoted on the war, "I believe the second coming of Christ is very close, so this is exciting to me personally, although of course I don't want anybody to die."[1]

Apocalyptic literature responds to the present crisis by positing a near-future solution. But in what ways does this solution affect the lives of women? How are women to respond to the Apocalypse of John? There are, of course, as many ways for women readers to respond to the Apocalypse as there are women readers. A totalizing theory would be impossible, for the "truth" of the text of the Apocalypse is always subverting itself/always being subverted. I want to enter into the subversive action of being one reader of the Apocalypse, grounded in my time and context but drifting in a postmodern space that allows for multiple readings and multiple subversions.

Not all of postmodern readings are ethical or acceptable in terms of women's lives. The text of the Apocalypse allows space/s for women but there is growing debate about whether or not the representation of women in the Apocalypse is redeemable or reclaimable for women. I think it is possible to read for gender and politics at the same time, even though I am more optimistic that a purely political reading of the Apocalypse can be reconstructive on at least some levels in some contexts.

Elisabeth Schüssler Fiorenza is positive on both fronts, connecting a feminist reading with a political/liberationist reading. She suggests that women read and identify with the Apocalypse "because they read it as "common literature" with whose humanist values and visions they could identify" (1991:14). I began as one of those women readers, reconciling the violence and destruction, because the oppressed triumphed over the oppressor and a new just world was created. In reading for the gender codes in the text, I grew uneasy about this utopia. Reading for the "lives" of the females in the text exposes the deep misogyny of this vision of the end of the world.

Further, reading for gender in the text is political; politics and gender interface in the text. But ultimately, I do not find "humanist values and visions" in the Apocalypse. Of course, both male and female are silenced and destroyed in the Apocalypse. I want to focus on the clearly identified women in the text who are destroyed and on the general "apocalypse of women" brought about in the utopian vision of the New Jerusalem. By the "apocalypse of women" I mean the misogyny and disenfranchisement that are at the roots of gender relations, accompanied by (hetero)sexism and racism, along with violence, poverty, disempowerment, and fear. "Apocalypse" is the reveiling of women—the silencing and marginalizing of women. It is also the revealing of women in that it constructs their sexual natures in good or evil terms. The apocalypse of women is the ultimate "backlash" against women. And this apocalypse of women is the destruction of women as women, through rape or pornography or stereotyping or any part of the mind-body dichotomy.

How are women to respond to the Apocalypse? By first of all listening to the voices of women past and present who speak out of their own apocalypses, their own crises and visions of the future. The text of the Apocalypse, with its female archetypes of good and evil, virgin and whore, is an account of a political and religious and also gender crisis of the end of the first century CE. Women readers are to bring a heightened hermeneutic of suspicion to the reading of this biblical text. I want to examine in this chapter what this hermeneutic might look like in the face of the ongoing apocalypse of women.

RE-VEILING/UN-VEILING:
READING THE APOCALYPSE

Matilda Joslyn Gage begins her reading of the Apocalypse with this statement: "The Book of Revelation, properly Re-Veilings, cannot even be approximately explained without some knowledge of astrology. It is a purely esoteric work, largely referring to woman, her intuition, her spiritual powers, and all she represents" (in Stanton 1974:184). This wordplay on the meaning of the Greek title "apocalypse," usually translated as an uncovering, revelation, discovery, or unveiling, is curious. Are the symbols and mysteries seen as re-veiling/revealing all at once, that is, covering at the moment they uncover meaning? Catherine Keller relates her definition of apocalypse as follows:

> "Apocalypse" . . . means "to remove the veil"—supposedly of the unknown virgin bride at the moment of consummation. Thus the warrior's initiation by destruction, "lifting the corner of the universe and looking at what is underneath," rips the veil off of a mystery that never was hidden. The veil was the separation imposed by the fathers and the father of the fathers. Another aesthetic, one not freed from human empathy to the horrors of transcendent destruction, invites us to its beauty. (1990:81)

To unveil is to remove mystery. In Keller's description the veil modern societies have created is the patriarchal nuclear complex. To unveil is to face death and the machines of death. Keller relates, "*Facing* . . . turns out to be just what the warrior does not do, never did, and seeks with his apocalypse to avoid eternally" (67). To unveil is to face the whole.

Women have been socialized to fear such face-to-face encounters. Psychic numbing keeps the veil in place. The desire for the end of the world is questioned only by a few. The Apocalypse unveils, unmasks the desire for death, and for utopia. It also reveils, remasks the ethics of violence and destruction. Gloria Anzaldúa explores what an unveiling means in terms of "making face, making soul":

> Among Chicanas/*méxicanas*, *haciendo caras*, "making faces," means to put on a face, express feelings by distorting the

face—frowning, grimacing, looking sad, glum or disapproving. For me, *haciendo caras* has the added connotation of making *gestos subversivos*, political subversive gestures, the piercing look that questions or challenges . . . (1990:xv)

Making faces—at war, at patriarchy, at racism, at classism, at heterosexism, at destruction, at the desire for the violent consummation at the end of time, at the hope of freedom, at the hope of equality, at the dream of a better world—this facing is part of women's response to apocalypse. Unveiling means change.

THE POETICS AND POLITICS OF DESTRUCTION

. . . to the hard of hearing you shout, and for the almost-blind you draw large and startling figures. (Flannery O'Connor 1957:34)

As part of our sacred canon the Apocalypse is about dealing with the end of the world. The Apocalypse is the ultimate disaster, the final holocaust. The writing of the disaster takes place in what Blanchot calls our bruised and wounded space (1986:30 and 55). This space is the reserve of the memory of the past—of wars and prisons and Hiroshima. Blanchot comments: "It is not you who will speak; let the disaster speak in you, even if it be by your forgetfulness or silence" (1986:4). The Apocalypse has a way of speaking even when silenced or placed on the margins of the canon and the lectionary. Regardless of critical stance, this telling of the disaster intrigues the reader. The eschatological disaster is always right at the tip of consciousness.

Recent readings in the Apocalypse include studies in the historical and socio-political context, genre studies, literary analysis, and liberation readings. Both Adela Yarbro Collins and Elisabeth Schüssler Fiorenza focus on the social and literary context. Since they are the two dominant women scholars of the Apocalypse, I will focus on their readings as/of women, since they present the generally accepted views in the academy and ask the pertinent questions for women readers of the Apocalypse.

Women Reading the Apocalypse

In *Crisis and Catharsis* (1984) Adela Yarbro Collins accepts the information given by Irenaeus that a prophet and seer John wrote the Apocalypse at the end of Domitian's reign (95 or 96 CE). Persecution of Christians is not widespread at the end of the first century; rather, martyrdom is sporadic and localized, based on public indictment. Yarbro Collins calls the crisis in the Apocalypse a "perceived crisis," based on broader factors of Roman imperialism: taxation and the imperial cult, in particular (1984:chap. 3). The telling of the disaster and subsequent "happy ending" for God's chosen is cathartic for the reader. This tale of the destruction of the Roman Empire brings an emotional and psychological release of internalized frustration and disempowerment. For the reader/hearer the Apocalypse provides a prophetic hope for justice brought about by God's new order.

When Yarbro Collins reads for women in the text, she is also reading for history. The social context of women's lives in late first century Christianity can be discovered in the Apocalypse. Yarbro Collins focuses on Apoc 14:1-5, the description of the 144,000. The preparation of this all male group of holy warriors includes sexual purity. Yarbro Collins compares this scene in the Apocalypse with the fallen angels who lie with women in the Book of the Watchers (1 Enoch 1-36): "Sexual intercourse with women is a narrative emblem for earthly existence" (1984:112). Inherent in these purity laws is the exclusion of women and the conclusion that contact with women's bodies is dangerous. On the sexual purity of the 144,000 men "who have not defiled themselves with women" (Apoc 14:4), Yarbro Collins comments: "Such a remark reveals a complex set of emotions, involving perhaps hatred and fear both of women and one's own body" (1987:89).

To go further with this line of reasoning, in the Apocalypse the body of woman is marginalized (the Woman Clothed with the Sun and the Bride) or violently destroyed (Jezebel and the Whore). What is considered unclean and dangerous by the male hierarchy has to be placed outside the camp. Those on the inside—the inside of the Bride, the New Jerusalem—in this cultural system are all male.

Elisabeth Schüssler Fiorenza approaches the Apocalypse with greater suspicion in terms of finding any definite historical figures behind the symbols. She states, "I will therefore argue that Rev. must be understood as a poetic-rhetorical construction of an alternative symbolic universe that "fits" its historical-rhetorical situation" (1985:183). Schüssler Fiorenza is making the move toward more dialogue with literary and ideological studies, grounding her work in a political hermeneutic. The effect of the composition of the Apocalypse is cathartic and leads naturally to a more detailed literary analysis. Schüssler Fiorenza is concerned with the total effect of this text. She notes:

> Exegetes and theologians still have to discover what artists have long understood: the strength of the language and composition of Rev. lies not in its theological argumentation or historical information but in its evocative power inviting imaginative participation. (1985:22)

This participation comes from an examination of the "rhetorical situation." The Apocalypse has hermeneutical value in the contemporary situation "wherever a social-political-religious "tension" generated by oppression and persecution persists or re-occurs" (1985:199). The ethical choice of either Christ or Caesar pushed in the Apocalypse has been used by Daniel Berrigan, Ernesto Cardenal, and Alan Boesak to address the oppression of nuclear proliferation, the oppression of Nicaragua under Somoza's rule, and the apartheid system of South Africa, respectively. The Apocalypse is a cathartic text for Christians in oppressive systems.

Regarding this possibility of different responses to the Apocalypse, Schüssler Fiorenza relates the characterization of women in the text. Rome and Israel are portrayed by female figures, and the believers are called from desiring the Whore to desiring the Bride. Schüssler Fiorenza argues:

> Rev. engages the imagination of the contemporary reader to perceive women in terms of good or evil, pure or impure, heavenly or destructive, helpless or powerful, bride or temptress, wife or whore. Rather than instill "hunger and thirst for justice," the symbolic action of Rev. therefore can perpetuate

prejudice and injustice if it is not "translated" into a contemporary "rhetorical situation" to which it can be a "fitting" response. (1985:199)

This response to the portrayal of women in the Apocalypse is similar to that of Yarbro Collins. A hermeneutic of suspicion is utilized to unveil the dialectic of the female. Schüssler Fiorenza argues for both a "feminist-liberationist strategy of rhetorical reading" in asserting ". . . the interpreter's agency, subjecthood, contextuality, particularity, stance, and perspective when reading Revelation" (1991:13). She wants to engage the text at the level of reconstruction rather than deconstruction.

Schüssler Fiorenza's argument concerning the male identity of the 144,000 is helpful: "A literal ascetic interpretation is unlikely since such a misogynist stance is nowhere else found in the New Testament" (1981:139). She chooses to focus on the overall liberating effect of the book rather than on gender, and this move rightly includes concerns of race, class, colonialism, and ethnicity (1991:14).

In her most recent book Schüssler Fiorenza takes issue with the reading I am advocating:

> The first feminist strategy of reading takes the androcentric, linguistic-cultural, sex/gender system as a self-contained, closed system signifying reality. . . . It does not, however, challenge this cultural androcentric perspective of reality; but by elaborating its sex/gender inscriptions, it reinscribes this system as a self-contained totality. Such an interpretation seeks to make readers conscious of internalized male identifications, but it cannot reclaim cultural texts and traditions for women. . . . If [readers] borrow critical methods and theories that valorize the sex/gender system and grid of reading, they risk magnifying the androcentric marginalization, objectification, alienation, and negation of women inscribed in the text. (1991:13-14)

The gender assumptions of the Apocalypse are not acceptable to twentieth century feminists, but Schüssler Fiorenza wants to transcend these gender assumptions. When she states that "interpreters must adopt methods and approaches that undermine the androcentric-reality construction of the text" (1991:

14), I could not agree more. But first the text must be allowed to speak. The inscribed negation of women is not something that can be worked out or generalized; oppression is always specific and specific females in the text are targeted, and this violence has impact on the specific lives of women readers by promoting an extreme hatred of women.

Before women "translate" the Apocalypse, the original representation of women in the text needs to be examined. The making of archetypes of the female and the abuse of women's bodies reveal a deep misogyny. Misogyny in the end of the twentieth century may be more technologically advanced, but the roots and results of woman-hatred are the same.

Schüssler Fiorenza and Yarbro Collins both provide positive readings of this canonical text. The feminist reading I am doing in this book sees women as marginalized (the woman left in exile in Apoc 12) and/or used as sexual objects and abused (Jezebel, the Whore, and the Bride). This blatantly misogynist text has one advantage for contemporary readers; the reader is facing the sexism that developed into the exclusion of women from positions of equality and power in the early (and later) church.

Decolonizing Apocalyptic

As an elite female embedded in a system of white privilege, I am able to focus my attention on the sexism of the Apocalypse. The ideology of gender in the text is a neglected area in studies on the Apocalypse, so a focus on gender and misogyny is partially justified by the history of the neglect of these topics. But in this reading for gender I am promoting a western, white feminist reading and hermeneutic. Gender oppression has to be linked with other forms of oppression that women experience. Since I am not third world[2] or living in poverty or in the midst of war, my voice is limited. In my gender analysis of the Apocalypse I cannot claim to speak for any women readers of this text except myself.

The majority of women suffer multiple oppression—sexism, racism, ableism, classism, ageism, heterosexism, colonialism. I am not listing these oppressions just to be "politically correct."

Rather, I am called by women of color to face my own role in their multiple oppressions and our mutual enslavement. Gayatri Spivak's focus on the oppressed or non-elite "people" as "subaltern" (from Italian Marxist Antonio Gramsci) draws attention to the role of the intellectual/elite in cultural and political oppression (1988:283). The hegemonic relation is exposed.

Spivak understands this hegemonic relationship as follows: "The subaltern cannot speak. There is no virtue in global laundry lists with "woman" as a pious item. Representation has not withered away. The female intellectual as intellectual has a circumscribed task which she must not disown with a flourish" (1988:308). There is no universal experience of women reading the Apocalypse. The voices that have been made Other or have been silenced—both in the fictional universe of the narrative and outside by the real readers of the text—have to be heard, have to be spoken to. The Apocalypse speaks to the subaltern who suffered the economic and political effects of economic and political domination.

When speaking of this oppression, the powerful lines of George Orwell's *1984* come to mind: "War is peace/Freedom is Slavery/Ignorance is strength" (5). Colonization brought about a heightened sense of apocalyptic times for the conscienticized. Many chose not to face the multiple oppression brought about by imperial policy: the economic hardships and extreme poverty in both urban and rural areas; the system of taxation and imposition by the local indigenous elite of the imperial cult; the presence of the military and politicos. The Apocalypse represents a minority view, or at least a view actively held by a minority of the colonized.

Thus, it is easy to see the immediate connections third world Christians make with the Apocalypse's response to oppression. Two comments by Alan Boesak serve as an example of the use of this text: "The Apocalypse is determined to keep the dream of God alive for God's people. It is a protest against and a call for resistance to evil. It depicts the dream of a new creation . . ." (1987:35). Boesak continues:

What we are learning is the truth that in order for a new South Africa to be born, we have to be willing to give up our lives. We are learning the meaning of the reply to the souls underneath the altar. And in the process we have exposed the true nature of the South African state. Their only power is the power to destroy. They can never last. (1987:83-84)

The Apocalypse becomes a decolonizing text.

It is difficult to read this ancient text for race and ethnicity, since the understandings of race were different in the Mediterranean basin of the ancient world, and inclusion in the "people of God" was based on covenant and not race. What is clear is that the 144,000 is an exclusive group. The outsiders of the imperial power, the colonized and Christian, become the insiders. As Yarbro Collins notes, ". . . the ultimate insiders were the Roman citizens" (1985:188).[3] This reversal of power and status is connected with the defeat of Babylon by God's army and the replacement of the throne of Babylon with the throne of God and the Lamb (Apoc 22:3).

The boundaries of the new covenant group are clear. Those people and groups not included in the covenant but mentioned in the text are "the cowardly, the faithless, the polluted, the murderers, the fornicators, the sorcerers, the idolaters, and all liars" (Apoc 21:8). Again: "Outside are the dogs and sorcerers and fornicators and murderers and idolaters, and everyone who loves and practices falsehood" (Apoc 22:15). Inside the heavenly city are the faithful. As the unfaithful are known by the mark of the beast on their foreheads, the people of God have God's seal on their foreheads. The 144,000 come from every tribe of Israel (Apoc 7:4-8). They represent the whole number of God's people, but they do not represent the Jews.

Along with the 144,000 is a countless group of redeemed: "After this I looked, and there was a great multitude that no one could count, from every nation, from all tribes and all peoples and languages, standing before the throne and before the Lamb, robed in white, with palm branches in their hands" (Apoc 7:9). Are the redeemed then culturally diverse? I think the answer to this question is both yes and no. Yes, there are all nations and tribes and languages represented in the multitude.

But no, only one religion is represented; there is no room for Jews or pagans or anyone who refuses to acknowledge the divinity of Jesus.

Yarbro Collins notes: "In Revelation, idolatry is focused on a goddess, Roma" (1985:214). A female is the receptacle of evil. It is of course impossible to separate the political from the religious; nonetheless, the idolatry of colonialism is tied with worship of the Goddess. For all the people (male and female) not in the covenant of God the judgment is severe: "their place will be in the lake that burns with fire and sulfur, which is the second death" (Apoc 21:8).

The boundary of the redeemed sets up a system of opposites expressed as insider and outsider, Christian and non-Christian, and fornicators and virgins. There is no room for dissent and no place for women's power and women's voices. The call to "patient endurance" (Apoc 1:9) in the midst of suffering has always been bad news for women. Only certain ones of the marginalized will be included in the inside. The demand for purity in the heavenly city means that any "other" religion is dangerous.

The global dialogue and movement toward multiculturalism in the late twentieth century demands a breaking of these cultural boundaries. Difference is not affirmed in the Apocalypse; everyone is called to be the same, regardless of their nation, tribe, or language. The Apocalypse has an oppressive function in women's lives. This text encourages exclusivity and protectionism, rather than an openness to and sharing of different religious traditions. The Apocalypse is decolonizing literature that turns around and recolonizes. A feminist reading of this text is necessarily deconstructive; the Apocalypse is made up of conflicting readings that cannot be resolved.

4

THE (W)HOR(E)ROR
OF IT ALL:
THE IDEOLOGY
OF DEATH

And I saw a woman sitting on a scarlet beast that was full of
blasphemous names, and it had seven heads and ten horns.
The woman was clothed in purple and scarlet, and adorned
with gold and jewels and pearls, holding in her hand a golden
cup full of abominations and the impurities of her fornication;
and on her forehead was written a name, a mystery: "Babylon the great, mother of whores and of earth's abominations."
And I saw that the woman was drunk with the blood of the
saints and the blood of the witnesses to Jesus. (17:3b-6)

The narrator of the Apocalypse of John relates a marvelous
feeling on encountering the Whore of Babylon. The female has
seductive power. The desire of the male who views her erotic
power is brought quickly under control by the angel: "Why are
you so amazed? I will tell you the mystery of the woman, and of
the beast with seven heads and ten horns that carries her"
(17:7). The desire is controlled by the angel's explanation of the
Whore and the beast and the scene of her violent death and
destruction. "And the ten horns that you saw, they and the
beast will hate the whore; they will make her desolate and
naked; they will devour her flesh and burn her up with fire"
(17:16).

There is a strong ascent-descent structure here. The object
of desire is made the object of death. The Whore/Goddess/
Queen/Babylon is murdered (a sexual murder) and eaten and

burned. This grotesquely exaggerated vision of death and desire accentuates the hatred of the imperial power—and of women. This story of death and desire is the most vividly misogynist passage in the New Testament. The Apocalypse is cathartic on many levels, but in terms of an ideology of gender, both women characters in the narrative and women readers are victimized.

The themes of death and desire are integral to the ideology of the text. The ideology of death and desire is a consuming part of the narrative—traceable from the key question in Apoc 5:2 ("Who is worthy to open the scroll and break its seals?") to the pronouncement in 5:12 ("Worthy is the Lamb that was slaughtered to receive power and wealth and wisdom and might and honor and glory and blessing!") to the humiliating death and funeral of the two witnesses (chapter 11) and of the Whore of Babylon (chapters 17-18), to the final utopian vision of the New Jerusalem. A reading attentive to ideology uncovers the "play of the subtext"—the play of power relations and gender relations. The play culminates as the power of God and the Lamb is reproduced in a violent enactment of the utopian future.

What does it mean to participate in the ideology of the text? In other words, what does it mean to examine "the way the text works as a signifying process which inscribes ideology?" (Greene/Kahn 1985:25). A Marxist-feminist reading stresses both women's experiences as readers and women's connection with the reproduction of power. The ideological structures of class oppression can be seen through both the presence of women in the text and the presence of women readers. In desiring utopia the gender oppression is overlooked. This dialogue between Marxism and feminism is a necessary challenge to the "strategies of containment" of traditional biblical scholarship. A political reading of the biblical text (here the Apocalypse) is capable both of opening the blank scroll of women's material lives and values and of producing a feminist ideology of reading.

Within the matrix of Marxist-feminist reading strategies, I am proposing a materialist-feminist reading of the Apocalypse of John. A materialist-feminist approach reads the story of the desire for and death of the Whore of Babylon along gender, racial/ethnic, and economic lines: the Whore is a woman *and* a foreigner *and* a wealthy foreign colonial oppressor. Such a reading incorporates both class and gender readings and de-centers the white-male-EuroAmericentric reading of the text. Judith Newton and Deborah Rosenfelt (1985:xxv) distinguish a materialist-feminist reading from traditional Marxist readings by "its emphasis on gender relations and on the transforming potential of white middle-class female desire" and "in its refusal to valorize that desire almost to the exclusion of other values." Thus, a materialist-feminist reading is involved in "the difficult task of exploring the changing relationships among ideas, language, and social conditions and relations" (Newton/Rosenfelt 1985:xxi). Reading in relation to the class struggle, economic conditions, and patriarchy pushes reading to the margins and incorporates the experiences of the marginalized in the reading process.

The Whore of Babylon is a mixed image. She is evil from the perspective of a traditional Marxist literary reading for class ideology, since she is responsible for diverse suffering linked with colonization. On the other hand, state power is embodied by a city represented by a woman, thus linking the evil with the female sex. The cathartic power of the death narrative has different levels of effect. The defeat of imperialism is reassuring but the defeat of the desire aroused by the splendor of Babylon is more ambivalent. The narrator's attraction is quickly averted by the angel. The boundaries of desire are drawn. The message is clear but strange: desire the Whore and you die; desire God and the Lamb and you will probably die as a martyr. The ultimate desire consummates in the desire for the Bride (New Jerusalem), where the martyr will resurrect and reside after death.

Women have always had a hard time with the figure of the prostitute in literature and life (see Horn and Pringle). The Whore is such an effective symbol because she divides women's emotions. The ideology of gender in the text reveals the choice of women readers of the Apocalypse—to identify with the Bride or the Woman Clothed with the Sun, but not the Whore or the Jezebel. A materialist-feminist reading reveals these textual/

sexual strategies for dividing the woman symbol in the narrative. Difference is not affirmed in the Apocalypse; the role and function of women is distinctly defined. So much textual space is spent on the death of the Whore, because she represents the opposition to women's true identity, at least according to the narrator. Newton and Rosenfelt (1985:xxix) are again helpful:

> A materialist-feminist analysis offers a more complex and in the end less tragic view of history than one polarizing male and female, masculine and feminist; constructing gender relations as a simple and unified patriarchy; and constructing women as universally powerless and universally good. A materialist-feminist analysis actively encourages us to hold in our minds the both-ands of experience: that women at different moments in history have been both oppressed and oppressive, submissive and subversive, victim and agent, allies and enemies both of men and one another.

The reader is thus seduced by the text of the Apocalypse. Using the narrative of the overthrow of the Whore as the central paradigm, there are several sexual/textual ideologies. The ideology of death—that death and martyrdom are valued and valuable for citizenship in the city of God—operates throughout the apocalyptic vision.

A comparison of the death of the two witnesses in Apocalypse 11 with the death of the Whore in chapters 17-18 reveals the basic ideology of death in the text and the effects these different deaths have on the reader. The ideology of gender includes the issue of reading the text as a woman, and links reader-response theories with materialist-feminist theories. The reproduction of power in the text is revealed by a materialist-feminist reading which defines power in gender terms—as erotic power—and which shows how erotic power is constructed and contained.

THE IDEOLOGY OF DEATH

The Apocalypse includes a mini-handbook within its pages—something like "Tragic Ways of Killing a Woman" (to borrow from Nicole Loraux). Loraux shows how the staging of women's deaths on the Greek stage brought both gender differences and the image of the body to the forefront. She states (1987:x), "Death by report lends itself to conjecture vastly more than does violence exposed to the public view." The tragic, or better, horrible death of the Whore is played in a fantastic, imaginative scene. The report of her death is enacted by many players and encourages audience participation.

Since the Whore is an example of what is known in literature as "the bitch-witch" (which resembles the *femme fatale* in her erotic power), she is joyfully destroyed. Pierre Horn and Mary Beth Pringle (1984:3) explain this literary archetype and the phenomenon of her death:

> The bitch-witch embodies wickedness and cruelty. She is a seductress who leads others to ruin or death, though authors seldom allow her to escape unscathed . . . . With few redeeming qualities, she leaves misery and destruction in her wake, until at last she is punished by a hideous illness, becoming the incarnation of a nightmare. One wonders about the deep well of misogyny from which such ghastly portrayals of the female surface. Because he fears and hates his own creation, the author who summons up the bitch-witch must destroy her before his work is finished.

In the Apocalypse the Whore is the embodiment of the evil of the imperial state. A woman bears the violent death. There is no "proper" funeral for the Whore; her body is publicly burned. Her followers lament from afar: first the kings lament (18:10), then the merchants lament twice (18:14-15 and 16-17), and finally the sailors lament (18:19-20).

They weep and mourn out loud, in a style typical of the Roman funeral lament. Keith Hopkins (1983:214) notes the typical parts of the urban Roman funeral: "paid mourners, sacrifices at the grave, a funeral banquet, a commemorative tomb." The funeral of the Whore has all of these components except the memorial tomb. But mourners do not eat over the body at the grave; they actually eat the body. They in turn are sacrificed and eaten by the birds of mid-heaven (19:17-21). The Whore is burned up and is no more, but those who are thrown into the lake of fire—the beast and the false prophet and Death and Hades—are thrown into the abyss, a symbol for a mass grave or a "collective pit" that was outside the city gates (Hopkins 1983:208). The funeral ceremony of the rich and powerful is parodied as a collective funeral for the poor of the Roman world. The rulers of the world all lose their identity in the mass grave. There is no memorial marker.

From heaven there is a different song: a song of thanksgiving and rejoicing over her death (18:21-24 and 19:1-8). This song of joy welcomes the Bride of Christ as the Whore's replacement. The funeral lament is followed by the wedding hymn: "'Let us rejoice and exult and give him the glory, for the marriage of the Lamb has come, and his bride has made herself ready; to her it has been granted to be clothed with fine linen, bright and pure'—for the fine linen is the righteous deeds of the saints" (19:7-8). The marriage ceremony and feast take place in heaven. When the Bride finally comes down from heaven, there is no more need for the funeral lament (weeping and pain). The pronouncement is made that "death will be no more" (21:4). A new order is established, but only after the oppressor experiences the second death (20:14; 21:8). Death is abolished in the New Jerusalem, the place of eternal life and light and wealth. Could the abolition of death be linked with the concept of evil and death brought to earth by Eve—and are all women being held responsible for death?

In Apocalypse 11 the death and funeral of the two witnesses are dramatized. Their death, like the deaths of all the martyrs, can be described as a "noble death." David Seeley's description (1990:91) of the noble death in Jewish (2 and 4 Maccabees), hellenistic, Roman, and Pauline writings is helpful here. The noble death consists of five main aspects, although these are not always present at the same time: "vicariousness, obedience, a military context, and overcoming physical vulnerability" and sacrifice. He further defines vicarious deaths in terms of mimeticism, using Eleazar's death in 2 Maccabees as an example, so that this "death provides others with a model or pattern for correct behavior" (145). Through the mimetic nature of Eleazar's death the people "reenact his death in their own imaginations. In mentally bearing the tortures he went through, they come to see that they, too, can win victory by endurance should they have to do so literally. An imaginative imitation prepares and strengthens them for the real thing" (145-146). The two witnesses in Apocalypse 11 have a mimetically vicarious function through their martyrdom. The reader imagines this martyrdom, dishonorable funeral, and ultimate vindication, and is given the strength and hope to endure should the situation arise.

Notice the power given, taken, and returned to the two witnesses. Initially, they are given the power to be prophets and magicians on a grand scale and work for "one thousand two hundred and sixty days" (11:3). They wear the sackcloth of repentance. "They have authority to shut the sky, so that no rain may fall during the days of their prophesying, and they have authority over the waters to turn them into blood, and to strike the earth with every plague, as often as they *desire*" (11:6). These two witness-martyrs obviously have violent desires! The text reports only that the two witnesses prophesy, and does not reveal whether or not they actualize this destructive power. This scene is juxtaposed with the preceding scene, in which the narrator eats the little scroll and is commissioned to prophesy "about many peoples and nations and languages and kings" (10:11). The two witnesses exemplify this prophecy and experience death at the hands of the beast.

At the end of their testimony the two witnesses are killed. In both the death and funeral descriptions the emphasis is on their bodies: "and their dead bodies will lie in the street of the great city" (11:8) and "for three and a half days members of the peoples and tribes and languages and nations gaze at their dead bodies and refuse to let them be placed in a tomb" (11:9). Their bodies are put on public display inside the gates of the city. The ultimate public humiliation is that they are left in the street and are refused a tomb or proper burial service. Instead of the typical funeral lament of mourning, the inhabitants "gloat over them and celebrate and exchange presents, because these two prophets had been a torment to the inhabitants on the earth" (11:10). The funeral service is again parodied.

The dead bodies are at the center of the narrative. They suffer humiliation for three and a half days; they are left in the street to rot. The dead bodies are symbols that initiate what Victor Turner (1969) calls liminality, by which the social roles of a community are reversed, leading to social and moral transformation (*communitas*). The witnesses are known by their bodies; God is present in voice and breath. God breathes life into the witnesses, and they stand up, greatly surprising the celebrating onlookers. After the witnesses are taken up into heaven in a cloud, a great earthquake follows, "and a tenth of the city fell; seven thousand people were killed in the earthquake, and the rest were terrified and gave glory to the God of heaven" (11: 13). Not death but the power of the resurrection and its aftermath bring fear in this scene.

The centrality of the body is brought out in the death and funeral scenes of the Whore and the two witnesses. In both instances the corpse is liminal. Both deaths are followed by the deaths of the funeral participants. Both deaths are accompanied by songs of thanksgiving at the victory of God. But on the stage of the Apocalypse the deaths are gender-specific. The deaths of women (Jezebel and the Whore) are horrible deaths that destroy their sexuality and seductiveness. The Woman Clothed with the Sun and the Bride are not killed, but their erotic power is controlled.

Terry Eagleton (1990:270) writes of Freud's concept of the death drive, or *Thanatos*, which is the antagonist of *Eros*: "The death drive, which lurks within our aggressivity, is thus tricked out of its nefarious intentions and harnessed to the business of establishing a social order." Thus, the relation between law and desire becomes paradoxical; this is "the history of desire in its great debate with authority" (Ricoeur quoted in Eagleton 1990:284). Martyrdom in the Apocalypse reveals this paradox of law and desire in the death drive. A new social order is created in the utopian vision, but as God's law unfolds in the narrative, the desire for the Whore remains strong. The tension this creates is never fully resolved in the Apocalypse. The symbols of the pregnant woman and the Bride as the city of God only accentuate that tension. Sexual desire is transferred to the virgin-bride-mother figure.

THE WHORE

In the Hebrew Bible the harlot is sometimes characterized as a heroine (Tamar in Genesis 38; Rahab in Joshua 2 and 6). But the loose woman of the Proverbs is depicted as a deceiver and a foreigner. In the Apocalypse the Whore, whose name on her forehead (a sign of slavery) is Babylon, is the "mother of whores and of earth's abominations" (17:5). She is the ultimate deceiver and "loose woman." The Whore is seductive; she is adorned in fine clothes and jewels and sits upon a scarlet beast. But looking closer, the golden cup is full of the evil of her sexual acts with the kings of the earth. "God remembered great Babylon and gave her the wine-cup of the fury of his wrath" (16:19). And she is "drunk with the blood of the saints and the blood of the witnesses to Jesus" (17:6). The scene of the Whore is extremely grotesque; she is a huge, exaggerated presence who is "seated upon many waters" (17:1). As in chapter 12 the setting for this vision is the wilderness, but in this scene the female is brutally murdered.

The thoughts of the Whore are revealed in 18:7: "Since in her heart she says, 'I rule as a queen; I am no widow, and I will never see grief.'" The belief in and expression of the powers of women are remnants of ancient belief in the Mother Goddess. Bottigheimer (1980:12) comments, "the female's original access to power through her association with nature became perverted and denied, so that more recent versions of fairy tales [i.e., Grimms'] relegate power held by females to the old, the ugly, and/or the wicked." The Whore declares herself a queen, and because of her egotism she is judged and destroyed.

The destruction of the Whore is violent and total. This fantastic scene is played on a grand scale; it is a "parody" of the dominant social, political, economic, and religious systems. The dialogical model of Mikhail Bakhtin is useful in reading this fantastic scene. As Rosemary Jackson (1981:36) summarizes:

> Unlike the marvelous or the mimetic, the fantastic is a mode of writing which *enters a dialogue with the "real" and incorporates that dialogue as part of its essential structure.* To return to Bakhtin's phrase, fantasy is "dialogical", interrogating single or unitary ways of seeing.

65

Bakhtin's formalist ties show that language is subversive; the dominant ideology is "interrogated" in fantasy. The form (genre) of this discourse is the Menippean satire (a comic genre in classical Greece), which Bakhtin (1984:127) finds as an example of parody. By parody Bakhtin means, "the creation of a *decrowning double*; it is that same "world turned inside out" . . . it was like an entire system of crooked mirrors, elongating, diminishing, distorting in various directions and to various degrees." Bakhtin finds menippea in the New Testament (gospels, Acts, and Apocalypse) but notes that the "dialogic element of the menippea" is expressed in the relations of opposites (good and evil) and thereby managed (1984:135).

Parody is located in the genre of the carnivalesque. The carnival is used in folklore to express a "serio-comical" approach to the world (Bakhtin 1984:108). Bakhtin reveals three main characteristics of the genre of the serio-comical: (1) the time of the narrative is the present reality; (2) the narrative is based on history and not legend, relying on "experience . . . and on free invention;" (3) the narrative has multiple levels. In Bakhtin's words:

> Characteristic of these genres are a multi-tone narration, the mixing of high and low, serious and comic; they make wide use of inserted genres—letters, found manuscripts, retold dialogues, parodies on the high genres, parodically reinterpreted citations; in some of them we observe a mixing of prosaic and poetic speech, living dialects and jargons . . . are introduced, and various authorial masks make their appearance . . . And what happens here, as a result, is a radically new relationship to the word as the material of literature. (1984:108)

This "carnival sense of the world" as both comic and serious is found in Christian narrative. Bakhtin (135) gives the example of "the scene of crowning and decrowning" Jesus as King of the Jews in the Gospel narrative. The scene of the fall of Babylon is also directly carnivalesque. The Whore, all adorned on the scarlet beast, and considering herself a queen, is dethroned. The narrator tells us of the erotic image of the Whore as queen: "When I saw her, I was greatly amazed"

(17:6). This mock coronation/decoronation scene is a communal ritual event which is performed in the public square and streets. Bakhtin describes the significance of this ritual:

> Carnival is the festival of all-annihilating and all-renewing time . . . this is not an abstract thought but a living sense of the world, expressed in concretely sensuous forms (either expressed or play-acted) of the ritual act. Crowning/decrowning is a dualistic ambivalent ritual, expressing the inevitability and at the same time the creative power of the shift-and-renewal, the *joyful relativity* of all structure and order, of all authority and all (hierarchical) position . . . Birth is fraught with death, and death with new birth. (1984:124-125)

Through the carnival ritual the masquerading queen is stripped of her power (cf. Francisco O. García-Treto 1992:153-71). The dominant ideology of power and oppression is overthrown. The mixture of poetry and prose provides a powerful sense of the eccentricity of the Whore and helps bring about the shift in the structures of authority.

The horrible carnival death of the Whore is expressed in vivid terms: "And the ten horns that you saw, they and the beast will hate the whore; they will make her desolate and naked; they will devour her flesh and burn her up with fire" (17:16). Bakhtin (1984:126) finds the image of fire ambivalent in carnival: "It is a fire that simultaneously destroys and renews the world." Three times (17:16; 18:8, 9) her burning is mentioned, and once we read that she will burn forever (19:3); three times it is mentioned that the destruction occurs in one hour (18:10, 17, 19).

In this scene the erotic tension is heightened; the Whore is literally stripped naked of her fine garments and jewels. Nakedness equals helplessness. Like the dragon goddess Tiamat in the Enuma Elish, the Whore is disembodied. The erotic tension here points to the ultimate misogynist fantasy! All the world's hatred of oppression is heaped on the Whore. Although the Roman Empire is not a scapegoat, the female is a scapegoat symbol: "With such violence Babylon the great city will be thrown down, and will be found no more" (18:21). The people at the carnival (the ten horns and the beast) "devour her flesh" (17:

16), and the violent feast image is repeated in chapter 19 when the birds of midheaven are called to "Come, gather for the great supper of God, to eat the flesh of kings, the flesh of captains, the flesh of the mighty, the flesh of horses and their riders, and the flesh of all, both free and slave, both small and great . . . and all the birds were gorged with their flesh" (vv. 17-18; 21). These two grotesque feasts frame the marriage supper of the Lamb in 19:9. The menu of the marriage supper is not given.

Everything is turned inside out in this carnival: the Whore is "drunk with the blood of the saints and the blood of the witnesses to Jesus" (17:6 and 18:24); the nations are drunk from fornicating with the Whore; the nations in turn feast on the Whore's desolate body (and in the process lose all their delicacies; 18:11-17; and finally, the birds of heaven feast on the nations. With the death of the Whore, the Bride "has made herself ready" (19:7) and "to her it has been granted to be clothed with fine linen, bright and pure"—for the fine linen is the righteous deeds of the saints" (19:8). This rebirth after the death of the Whore is a sexual rebirth, or at least a rebirth in sexual imagery (the marriage feast). The witch is burned (the hunting of the Whore is a form of witch hunt), and the heroine image is finally free.

5

FANTASY
AND THE
FEMALE:
THE IDEOLOGY
OF DESIRE

Any sexist work (whatever "sexist" might mean, and whatever other qualities the sexist work might have) is flawed.

— Wayne Booth
(on Rabelais)

The erotic is the realm in which the spiritual, the political and the personal come together.

— Starhawk

There is only desire and the social, nothing else.

— Gilles Deleuze

In responding to science fiction writer Joanna Russ, Robert Scholes (1981:87) states, "Maybe an all-female world is the only hope for the future of the human race. It's worth considering." Women readers of the Apocalypse of John may entertain a similar idea. In the Apocalypse the earth-bound females (Jezebel and the Whore of Babylon) are immoral and seductive, and help the evil men to destroy earth. Only the Woman Clothed with the Sun is able to function positively in bringing about the utopia, but even she is left out of the utopian city (represented by the Bride). The role of the female is subordinate in the text; once women are used or abused they are either denied a place in the future world or their future function is left undefined.

The thesis of this chapter is that in the Apocalypse women are disempowered in every way, especially in the erotic dimension. Female desire is displaced and controlled. The social construction of gender in the Apocalypse leaves the female body as the object of male desire.

Reading the text as a woman demands reading for the gender codes in the narrative where women appear or are noticeably absent. If Joanna Russ (1972) is correct in her analysis of science fiction, there are no women, only "images of women." The female in fantasy literature is also an image; in the Apocalypse this image is blurred or stereotyped when present, or else it is absent altogether. Women are either on "the edge of time" (to borrow from Marge Piercy) or completely displaced from time.

In the enchanting and disenchanting world of the Apocalypse the role of the female is overlooked. Displacement occurs in the political and religious spheres. But women are displaced twice—they are "double-bound" to subordinate roles in both worlds. As seen earlier, the apocalyptic text reveals and displaces two main female archetypes: the Whore and Jezebel. The positive women symbols (the Woman Clothed with the Sun and the Bride) are also displaced. Studies in fantasy literature, folktales, and fairytales provide interesting parallels to the apocalyptic imagination. The text of the Apocalypse subverts the status quo without changing the gender relations and without empowering the "collective female."

Women are most noticeably absent in the Apocalypse in 14.4: "It is these who have not defiled themselves with women, for they are virgins." The 144,000 represent the whole number of the faithful, and they are all men. Adela Yarbro Collins (1987:84-90) notices that this passage employs sacrificial language and reflects purity laws. Women's bodies are seen as negative and capable of defiling the men, and hints that this passage "assumes that the model Christian is male" (90), but she fails to make full use of the logical inference—that the New Jerusalem, God's future world, will exclude females! For the candidates for heaven to remain "spotless"—indeed for heaven itself to remain spotless—women are displaced. "And in their mouth no lie was found; they are blameless" (14:5) removes the power of discourse from women. Male is the subject; female is the object—the object of desire that must be displaced.

Thus, the subject/object split is in place—that same split that is the dialectic of body/mind, nature/culture, and male/female. In the Apocalypse the narrative as "socially symbolic act" retains the sexual oppression and stereotypes of woman as object of violence and desire. As we have seen, a feminist hermeneutic rereads the narrative for its gender codes. A key question is who is the female and what are her powers and plays in the Apocalypse?

A tension exists in the narrative between the archetypes of the female. This dialectic of archetypal material can be explained by the subject-object split or in terms of binary oppositions or by the concept of displacement. The female that is displaced as subject in this political fantasy is the female that reflects (mirrors or mimics) aspects of the prevailing social order (both good and evil) and ideology. Lance Olson's definition of postmodern fantasy clarifies the deconstructive mode of fantasy literature:

> Often fantasy begins in the realm of the mimetic, then disrupts it introducing an element of the marvelous, the effect being to jam marvelous and mimetic assumptions. In other words, fantasy is that stutter between two modes of discourse which generates textual instability, an ellipse of uncertainty . . . its result is the banging together of the *here* and *there* so that neither the reader nor the protagonist knows quite where he is. That is, fantasy is a deconstructive mode of narrative. (1987:19)
>
> Hence, fantastic is a mode designed to surprise, to question, to put into doubt, to create anxiety, to make active, to make uncomfortable, to disgust, to repel, to rebel, to subvert, to pervert, to make ambiguous, to make discontinuous, to deform. It is a mode whose premise is a will to deconstruct. (1987:22)

The Apocalypse has elements of both the supernatural (Todorov's "marvelous") and the mimetic. And the narrative certainly subverts "reality" of the power relations. But the images of the female remain the same as in the dominant society—only in the reverse; the images are turned inside-out. The Apocalypse falls short of complete subversion of the social order. The female is still absent, even though she is represented in both powerful and powerless modes of being and acting. The female is still other, still marginalized, and still banished to the edges of the text.

As noted in the previous chapter, females in the Apocalypse are few but noticeable, and their future is prophesied. The prophetess Jezebel and her unrepentant followers will be thrown upon a sickbed and will die (2:22-23). The Whore of Babylon is dethroned and made desolate and totally destroyed, as the ceremonial lines proclaim: "Fallen, fallen is Babylon the great" (18:2). Even the Woman Clothed with the Sun is "banished" for protection and safekeeping to the wilderness "to her place where she is to be nourished for a time, and times, and half a time" (12:14). The female becomes the absent cause—the cause of both evil and good—erased from the text.

The bride image (the New Jerusalem) alone is left standing, but only briefly; she is replaced by the imagery of the city.[1] The final female image is connected with a male, the Lamb, and described as "prepared as a bride adorned for her husband" (21:2). The Bride is woman as object, adorned and passive; the New Jerusalem is the image of the seductive, the object of erotic desire. I want to show that all the females in the Apocalypse are victims; they are objects of desire and violence because they are all stereotyped, archetypal images of the female rather than the embodiment of power and control over their own lives in the real or fantastic worlds.

The language of female subjection and displacement in the Apocalypse comes out of the unconscious. And the unconscious is part of the imaginary order. Imagination is not fixed but fluid. The unconscious desire for the new social and political order does nothing to improve the status of women. The imaginary is ideological (Althusser), and the ideology of gender types in the text is controlled by the sexual imagination of the male. The imagination operating in the text involves the image of the virginal male controlling the female images. This is a result of the hierarchal order: God and the Lamb, the 144,000 males, the good female images, and the evil female images along with those males who are seduced by them. The desire of the true believer is to enter the heavenly city (the Bride). But there is erotic tension at this point; there is distancing from the female; entrance into the female is future and is possible only if the group of men desiring her remain sexually pure and undefiled by women. The vision is real; the world of the unreal becomes real in fantasy literature.

Studies on women in science fiction have revealed the powerlessness of women in the future world. The male remains the paradigm and subject of the future. One such study (Allen/Paul:171) relates that women function as sexual beings and "as appropriate rewards for the male protagonists who solve the problem. When a woman acts independently, she is evil; when she has power, it is intuitive or magical; when she has extra-human abilities, they are the problem." The granting of magical abilities in the Apocalypse must come from God or the Lamb; women who act on their own are defying the male-defined sex roles for women. Thus, the Jezebel and the Whore are destroyed, but the real point is that these autonomous females are "scapegoats" for the evil in society. Evil is again associated with the female and with her body.

The female with power is both desired and feared. The threat of a female with power over men—power identified in the form of seduction—is so feared that the reaction is violence against the female. Unconscious (or conscious) desire for the powerful, autonomous female remains even after she is destroyed. The image is still implanted on men's minds; in the Apocalypse this desire is transferred to the Bride. Coming out of the Whore and entering the Bride is set up as a rite of undefiled men, but the sexual fantasy is strong and luring. The Bride lures the 144,000; the adorned Bride is an enchanting and erotic image. All the apocalyptic females are erotic images with erotic power over men.

The erotic, enchanting female brings either death or birth. The either/or nature of the political stance in the Apocalypse is clear, but here I want to further this claim to the sexual images.

The distinct female archetypes represent either the way to God (rebirth in the New Jerusalem) or the way to Satan (death in the abyss). Donald Palumbo (1986:4) makes an interesting point about the "connection between eroticism and death." Our subconscious fears of the unknown (especially death) are made available to us in fantasy literature; fantasy overcomes death. Palumbo believes that the concern of the fantastic with sexuality gives it "psychological appeal." He summarizes his findings: "And sexuality almost always appears as the symbolic vehicle of rebirth in the nearly ubiquitous death and resurrection motifs that suffuse great fantasy literature" (23).

Fear of imperialism, fear of famine, fear of disease, even fear of death itself, are infused into the archetype of the seductive Whore whose erotic power over men is the most terrifying in a society that marginalizes and disempowers females. Females with autonomous power bring death. Only those females who are connected with God—adorned for the honeymoon or with wombs for use by God—that is, brides and mothers (men-identified women), are safe. These are women who are controlled by men and who do not exercise their powers independently. Still, they too lure men; they are also highly erotic images of desire. And the images of bride and queen-mother are intended to be more erotic, more desirable and enchanting, than the images of prophetess and whore.

THE HEROINE

> A great portent appeared in heaven: a woman clothed with the sun, with the moon under her feet, and on her head a crown of twelve stars. (12:1)

The Woman Clothed with the Sun in Apocalypse 12 is so historicized that she has almost lost her place as a character in her own right in the story. Like the Bride and the Whore who represent cities, she is seen as representing institutions; namely, Israel and the Church. But unlike the other female figures in the text, the Woman Clothed with the Sun has no name. Her fate is undetermined (although we assume she is safe), whereas the fate of the others is explicitly stated. She is set against a formidable foe, the great red dragon, but with help (from God), she is able to escape. She is speechless except for her cries of pain in childbirth. And she is overlooked—barely visible—since traditionally the battle between God and Satan has overshadowed her importance in the text.

If readings of the Grimms' *Kinder-und Haus Märchen* and other folk and fairytales are any indication, then the reader's identification (especially if the reader is a woman) is with the heroine in a story. Karen Rowe (1979:237) offers an explanation for this heroine identification:

> Thus, subconsciously women may transfer from fairy tales into real life cultural norms which exalt passivity, dependency, and self-sacrifice as a female's cardinal virtues. In short, fairy tales perpetuate the patriarchal *status quo* by making female subordination seem a romantically desirable, indeed an inescapable fate.

The implications of this mother archetype is that the female as a sexual being is affirmed only in the act of giving birth (to the Messiah, no less!): "And she gave birth to a son, a male child, who is to rule all the nations with a rod of iron" (12:5). In other words, the message is that females are productive only when they are reproductive.

The woman in Apocalypse 12 is identified twice by her reproductive event (12:5 and 13). The sexual affirmation of the Woman Clothed with the Sun in the birth process is in direct opposition to the orgy of the Whore and her followers.[2] Pain in childbirth is set against the pleasure of orgasm.[3] Sexual difference in the text points out the dialectic of desire; the text plays with the erotic on both sides (good and evil females) while reaffirming traditional stereotypes of the good woman who is obedient and long-suffering (emphasis on long).

In Apocalypse 12 the woman is connected with nature. Sun and moon and stars and wilderness evoke the natural order but also open the way to God. Yarbro Collins finds parallels between the Queen of Heaven in Apocalypse 12 and the goddesses Artemis (Ephesus), Atargatis (Syria), and especially Isis (Egypt and Asia Minor). Sun, moon, and stars (zodiac) are used in depictions of these goddesses. Yarbro Collins (1976:75) states, "The astral attributes with which she is endowed seem to

belong to the typical depiction of a high goddess." Another
detail of the goddess Isis that is shared by the woman in 12:14
is the giving of the wings. Isis is represented in the form of a
swallow who has power in flight. This is a typical image of the
goddess. The magical wings enable the woman to escape
danger and fly to the wilderness. The bird motif is a very powerful symbol of the high goddess, but the woman in chapter 12
is not allowed such status. The Whore is high goddess for
awhile, but she is brought down by the male god. Here is
another example, like the grotesque destruction of Tiamat in the
Enuma Elish, of the death of the goddess and her replacement
by the male god as head.

The female in this story does not get enough credit. She gives
birth on her own to the messiah child, who is immediately
snatched from her by God and taken up to heaven. Meanwhile,
the woman flees to the wilderness two times (12:6 and 14), and
she is left there. She enacts a kind of "travelling heroism" that
is evident in women characters of fantasy literature (Lefanu
1988:ch. 3), and thus is an active heroine, except that she does
not enact her own equality.[4] She takes the initiative in fleeing
to the wilderness and is cared for by God.

The Woman Clothed with the Sun is a goddess subdued,
tamed, and under control. After her reproductive activity she is
no longer useful. The traditional female values that accompany
the act of mothering (nurture and caretaking) are suppressed;
the child is taken to live in heaven, and traditional male values
of competition and separation come to the foreground. The
Woman Clothed with the Sun, Jezebel, and the Whore are all
hunted; only the Woman Clothed with the Sun escapes, but her
escape is banishment from the center of power. The female is
decentered even when held as an ideal woman.

Why the residue of Goddess/Queen of Heaven cults? If the
woman in Apocalypse 12 is the producer of the one who will
liberate the oppressed, then why is she not herself liberated?
The irony of the function of women in the Apocalypse is overwhelming. The Queen of Heaven is condemned to silence.

Silence has an interesting function for the females of the
Apocalypse. The model of the silent woman is a model for many

heroines in fantasy and folktale. According to Eugene Weber (1981:110), "it is not surprising that in a lot of folktales enduring in silence is one of the most common tests a heroine (or even a hero) has to pass, often connected with torment by witches or by devils." Ruth Bottigheimer (1987:71) finds that the majority of folktales in *Grimms' Märchen* condemn "women to silence during which they are often exposed to mortal danger," which is part of what Bottigheimer refers to as "textual silence and powerlessness" (53).[5]

The only sound of the mother of chapter 12 was her "crying out in birthpangs, in the agony of giving birth." Gloria Anzaldúa (1987:21) writes about the cultural power of women wailing:

> My Chicana identity is grounded in the Indian woman's history of resistance. The Aztec female rites of mourning were rites of defiance protesting the cultural changes which disrupted the equality and balance between female and male, and protesting their demotion to a lesser status, their denigration. . . . The Indian woman's only means of protest was wailing.

We hear the mother's anguish but not her words. Instead of words, she is given wings, "the two wings of the great eagle" (12:13). Still, she does not speak; she endures in silence in the wilderness. The voice of resistance is silenced. The two brief scenes of power where she flees and flies into the wilderness are quickly joined with scenes of dependency on the power of God as the ultimate protector. She is a goddess who has some power but needs to be saved, nonetheless, by a male god.

The textual/sexual strategies at work in the motif of the silent female are dangerous to women's consciousness. Female voice and values are suppressed.[6] Political and economic structures are subverted in the narrative, but women's roles and functions remain the same. The woman who "speaks," Jezebel, is vicious not virtuous. The archetyping of the female and her narrative silence relays a powerful message to the reader/hearer of the text: all women are to remain silent, but not all silent women are "good."

GODDESSES AND MONSTERS

A woman in the shape of a monster
a monster in the shape of a woman
the skies are full of them

— Adrienne Rich, "Planetarium"

A thinking woman sleeps with monsters.

— Adrienne Rich, "Snapshots of a Daughter-in-Law"

Part of the patriarchal politics of the Apocalypse is to focus on the so-called positive figures of women, the Woman Clothed with the Sun and the Bride. These are females who are controlled by the patriarchal politics and are made up and made passive. Along with the so-called evil women of the Apocalypse (Jezebel and the Whore), all these females represent some form of goddesses subdued and killed. Catherine Keller defines the key issue here: "The defeat of female "monsters" symbolizes the defeat of prepatriarchal modes of being, culturally, bodily and spiritually . . . Do these women, these goddesses, these metaphors of female energy, become monstrous because they threaten the masculinist separatism, threaten to prevent its coming to be in the first place?" (1990:76). The Apocalypse is about many things, but the death of goddesses looms large.

A student modelled these "good" and "evil" forms in a project on woman as virgin and whore in medieval art in a class of mine on early and medieval Christianity. Along with slides of representative art, this student dressed in the dichotomy: a sheet made into a toga tied over one shoulder with the other shoulder bare. Her face was divided by a line: one side was the virgin with the white face paint of a mime and hair pulled back (corresponding to the shoulder covered by the toga); the other side represented the whore with rouge and painted eyes and wild hair. What was striking about this portrayal was the split face, the binary opposition of good and evil all in one woman.

In artistic representations of the Whore in the Apocalypse she is a beautiful presence. Especially striking is the smiling Whore of Lovis Corinth's 1916 lithograph, "The Whore of Babylon." An angel trumpets while kings pull and eat hunks of flesh from the body of the Whore, who looks off to the side with an absent smile. This representation shows the subduing of the "erotic power" of women, along with the extreme fear of the power of women's bodies.

Carol Christ and others point to the symbol of goddesses as controlled and reimaged in terms of male power in both the virgin and whore archetypes. Christ states: "The simplest and most basic meaning of the symbol of the Goddess is the acknowledgment of the legitimacy of female power as a beneficent and independent power" (1987:121). The representation of the evil state (political and psychological) as female in the Apocalypse is no accident or anomaly. The Apocalypse is "the writing of the disaster" of the history of women in male-dominated societies. The death of goddesses signifies the death of women's power.

Yet there is some magic in the scene in Apocalypse 12 when the Woman Clothed with the Sun puts on the great eagle's wings and flies into the wilderness. The earth (Gaia) comes to the aid of the Woman—"it opened its mouth and swallowed the river that the dragon had poured from his mouth" (Apoc 12:16). The spiritual feminine is seen as subduing the material masculine. This view of the Woman is positive and helpful in revisioning goddesses in this powerful scene.

In all of these metaphors of the religious body as female goddesses are captured and subdued and molded (or in Apoc 12 is exiled) to fit male fantasies of the ideal female. The Bride is adorned as counter to the stripping and burning of the Whore. The marriage of the Bride counters the death/funeral of the Whore. The ancient goddess in all her characteristic diversity of motherhood, erotic sexuality, virginity, and as warrior, justice giver, caretaker, creatrix of nature and arts, and destroyer is segmented into these binary oppositions of good and evil, whore and virgin-mother. The Goddess is compartmentalized and stereotyped. Gloria Anzaldúa relates this fragmentation:

> You say my name is ambivalence? Think of me as Shiva, a many-armed and legged body with one foot on brown soil, one on white, one in straight society, one in the gay world, the man's world, another in the working class, the socialist,

and the occult worlds. A sort of spider woman hanging by one thin strand of web. Who, me confused? Ambivalent? Not so. Only your labels split me. (1981:205)

Anzaldúa calls for an end to the dominant ideology that determines the "ideal woman." She recalls that wild spirit of a goddess, freeing woman to make her own definitions about her body, her self, and her salvation.

The judgment on women is vicious in the Apocalypse. Women are left with no safe space. God's people are called out of the fallen city (the Whore) and into the new city, the New Jerusalem (the Bride). The love/hate relationship with the Whore is transferred to the Bride of Christ. The Bride is a beautiful virgin who marries the Lamb and becomes the heavenly city. The virginal 144,000 male followers of the Lamb are allowed to enter the Bride. This scene is disturbing because the imagery is that of mass intercourse. After the holy war all the blessed (men) partake in a double ecstasy: killing the enemy woman and sharing in the victor's spoils of war. Women in this narrative are not safe. They are killed or "prepared as a bride adorned for her husband" (Apoc 21:2). The female who is safe is in exile in the wilderness and is alone, her child taken from her. Women in the Apocalypse are victims—victims of war and patriarchy. The Apocalypse is not a safe space for women.

In effect I am saying that the Apocalypse is not liberating for women readers. This reading goes against the grain of traditional reconstructionist feminist hermeneutics. I find in the Apocalypse only negative and male-dominated images of women. This biblical text of the end of time is so misogynist that I continue to be shocked by its blatant voice. The maternal and bride images are often the points of redeeming this text for women, but both these images are patriarchal and heterosexist. In general, readings of the Apocalypse ignore the gender roles and focus on the political implications. A political reading using liberation theology does reveal the call to endurance and hope in the text, and this reading is important. Having studied the evils of Roman imperial policy in the colonies, I find the violent destruction of Babylon very cathartic. But when I looked into the face of Babylon, I saw a woman.

A reading for political codes in the text is not enough. In her writing on the Apocalypse Mary Daly explains: "No one asks *who* are the agents of wickedness. It is enough to have a scapegoat, a victim for dismemberment" (1990:105). I think the Apocalypse calls for multiple responses—of catharsis, of hope, of fear, and of horror.

The Apocalypse is an open text for finding some of the early roots of misogyny in the history of the Christian church. The function of this text in women's lives—both directly and indirectly—is especially vivid in the centuries of witch burning in Europe and North America. Those women with the ancient knowledge of midwifery and herbs and medicine and the religions of old Europe were seen as a threat. Even more, the *Malleus Malleficarum*, the fifteenth century text against witchcraft, makes the claim that witches had intercourse with demons and that women are more susceptible to the charms of the devil (Kraemer:1951). Note that the Whore is seated on a scarlet beast with seven heads and ten horns (Apoc 17:3) which finally all turn against the Whore: "they and the beast will hate the whore; they will make her desolate and naked; they will devour her flesh and burn her up with fire" (17:16). This image of fire became reality for women accused of witchcraft, a period of women's history Mary Daly refers to as "The Burning Times" (1990:216). Daly continues:

> . . . the technological true believers of the Book of Revelation live their fatal faith, the faith of the Fathers. Knowing their own rightness/righteousness, they are participant observers in the stripping, eating, and burning of the "famous prostitute," the whore hated by god and by the kings (leaders) he has inspired. The harlot "deserves" to be hated and destroyed, of course, for she symbolizes the uncontrollable Babylon, the wicked city. (1990:104-105)

As women readers of the Apocalypse and of the history of patriarchal politics and misogyny in Christianity, have we not been too willing participants in this scapegoating of the Whore? Have we not accepted too readily the ideal image put before women by the patriarchy? Have we not sung too enthusiastically the taunt song at the funeral of the Whore and the triumphant hymn of the entry of the pure, male believers into the heavenly city?

The Whore is totally seductive. The Whore totally dominates. In Apocalypse 18:4 a voice from heaven says, "Come out of her, my people, so that you do not take part in her sins, and so that you do not share in her plagues." The erotic power of the Whore is all-encompassing, for the people are asked to "come out of her." Then in 22:17 the word "come" is repeated to the believers: "The Spirit and the Bride say, "Come." And let everyone who hears say, "Come." And let everyone who is thirsty come. Let everyone who wishes [desires] take the water of life as a gift." The believers who come out of the Whore are able in the end to enter the New Jerusalem, to "come" into the Bride. Richard Kearney (1988:294-295) explains Derrida's comment on the significance of the word, "come."

> "Come" is a paradigmatic figure of postmodern apocalypse because it deconstructs every conceptual or linguistic attempt to *decide* what it means. It hails from an altogether *other* world. And what it puts into play is an apocalypse *without* apocalypse—since we cannot say or know or imagine what the "truth" of apocalypse means. Derrida thus confronts us with the word of an apocalyptic writing which can only be grasped, if at all, as an *ending without end* . . . What is to come is, apparently, beyond the powers of imagination to imagine.

The deconstructive play of apocalypse leaves the text open-ended and (temporally) shifts the object of desire (from the Whore to the Bride). The narrative itself is seductive, drawing the reader to the "ending without end"—the open spaces of the fantastic vision.

THE IDEOLOGY OF DESIRE

The concept of desire is immediately both a philosophical and a psychoanalytical concept; it can be traced through Plato, Aristotle, Hegel, Freud, Foucault, Deleuze, Lacan, Girard. The male definitions which have emerged have been critiqued by feminist theorists, especially Moi and Kristeva. The interplay of these theories of desire is mind-boggling; for purposes of reading a specific text here, I begin with Peter Brooks' statement (1984:61) on narrative desire in his analysis of plot:

> Narratives portray the motors of desire that drive and consume their plots, and they also lay bare the nature of narration as a form of human desire: the need to tell as a primary human drive that seeks to seduce and to subjugate the listener, to implicate him [sic] in the thrust of a desire that never can quite speak its name—never can quite come to the point—but that insists on speaking over and over again its movement toward that name.

The plot of the Apocalypse seduces the reader in its telling of the story. The movement is spiral (Schüssler Fiorenza), and for the reader the "thrust" into the future utopia is temporary and fleeting. Since only males and male readers thrust into the New Jerusalem, the desire of women and women readers remains unattended.

Susan Winnett (1990:506) criticizes Brooks (and Robert Scholes) for their male readings: "the pleasure the reader is expected to take in the text is the pleasure of the man" and "it would seem that the pleasure of the text depends on the gratification of the reader's erotic investment" (511). The male narrator shows his own erotic investment in the vision of the Whore and tells of the destruction of her body with great detail and repetition of her burning and being laid waste in only one hour. Women readers of the Apocalypse have faked pleasure so long they no longer even feel the text. A male myth of utopian desire has been created by men, and women who read the male myth are taught to read it as men. Women's roles are defined by men.

The roles of women in the male myth of the Apocalypse are virgin, whore, and mother—beloved and hated—but always under male control and domination. Tilde Sankovitch (1988:3-4) points out that when women appear in male myths they appear

> . . . in forms, figures, and images that are not hers, and do not reflect her adequately or accurately. When women show up in the books of male myths it is under names they themselves do not recognize, springing from an alien naming, and clad in deceptive images equally alien to what they gropingly know

and intuitively feel to be true about themselves . . . their presence is a mock presence. Women are really absent from them, since only false names, false icons, inane and without reverberation or deep radiance, pretend to represent women.

The Apocalypse is a phallocentric text that exploits these female images as part of male desire. The unconscious desires of the male reader, not only for the destruction of the dominant political and economic power but for the destruction of the sexual power of the female, are found in the ideology of desire in the text. Sankovitch writes further, "Sex—that is, what makes woman subservient to a patriarchal scheme of male desire and female reproductivity—is what defines her, not reason, imagination, or feeling, nor her own desire" (1988:2). The mother in Apocalypse 12 is a prime example of women's reproductive power being controlled by men. The war takes precedence, and the child is taken from her.

The ideology of desire is complex; there are conflicting desires in the Apocalypse. There is repressed desire for the female in the utopia without females. René Girard's (1977:146) concept of triangular or mimetic desire is helpful here. The triangle consists of subject and object and rival. Girard's basic statement is as follows: Desire is mimetic because the subject and the rival both desire the object. "Thus, mimesis coupled with desire leads automatically to conflict."

Toril Moi (1982:21) reveals Girard's essentially male reading of desire and shows how "Girard's theory of mimetic desire cannot account for feminine desire." The woman is the object of desire.[7] Subject-object-rival are a male trinity. In a Girardian reading of the Apocalypse Michael Harris (1988a:26) posits that "the Apocalypse is blind to its own mechanism of scapegoating." Since scapegoats and victims result from triangular desire, I want to posit that the scapegoat mechanism is transferred from the Lamb to the symbols of oppression (beasts and the dragon) and to the women who have seductive power (Jezebel, the Woman Clothed with the Sun, and the Whore—and the unnamed women who are excluded from the New Jerusalem). Men certainly die in the Apocalypse. But women are the double victims in this narrative.

Narrative desire has its base in discourse. What the narrator of the Apocalypse tells and does not tell—what the characters say and do not say—these are important variables for the "motor" of desire in the text. Speaking on Augustinian and medieval concepts of desire, Sarah Spence (1988:129) relates: "Desire has been reincorporated into the rhetorical act. In order to attain truth—in order to be converted or even persuaded—one must employ both reason and desire, the latter valorized as will . . . every act of oratory involves the willing participation of the audience." The rhetorical force of the Apocalypse is to persuade the readers/hearers to come out of the Whore and come into the Bride. The murder scene is political and sexual, and conflicting desires are managed and reduced to the one "true" desire—the desire for the male utopia.

Feminist reworkings of the psychoanalytic theorist Jacques Lacan further expose the operations of desire. To summarize, for Lacan "desire is the differential between demand and need . . . midway between silence and speech" but is always in a state of indeterminacy or contradiction (Butler 1987:198-199; cf. Goodheart 1991:ch. 7). The movement from Hegelian understandings of desire to the Lacanian concept "shifted the issue of literary emotion to the symbolic plane . . . *desire* ceased to be an affective term" (Oxenhandler 1988:115). Desire continually searches for the Other, so desire is never fulfilled.

For Elizabeth Grosz (1989:25), "In substituting the phallus for the penis, Lacan has provided a socio-cultural and political analysis in place of an ontological and biological one." Grosz also emphasizes the triangular nature of desire in Lacan, involving subject, other (object), and Other. In this drive of desire the Whore (object) is violently sacrificed. Woman becomes a monster who drinks the blood of the martyrs, and as Jane Gallop (1989:23) puts it, "the monster is the text's clitoris."

Desire is thus a social and political category in literature. In the Apocalypse the Monster/Whore is destroyed and replaced with the controlled and controllable image of the Bride. The Bride is passive and receptive to male authority and power. Judith Butler (1987:203) points to a "double-alienation" that occurs when female desire is displaced:

For Lacan, then, female desire is resolved through the full appropriation of femininity, that is, in becoming a pure reflector for male desire, the imaginary site of an absolute satisfaction. The "double-alienation" of the woman is a thus a [sic] double-alienation from desire itself; the woman learns to embody the promise of a return to a preoedipal pleasure, and to limit her own desire to those gestures that effectively mirror his desire as absolute.

The Whore is impure; the Bride is pure. The Whore is drunk with "the blood of prophets and saints" (18:24) and "all the nations have drunk the wine of her impure passion" (18:3a). Note that the Whore's passion is impure, and this impurity has a material base in the economic and political scene. The kings and merchants are the rich. They have gazed too long at the Whore.

"The politics of the gaze" (a phrase from Diane Hunter) relates to the death scene of the Whore. In gazing at the Whore the reader encounters imaginary desire in the text and is clearly shown the choices of death and eternal life. Meanwhile, the Bride dines at the eucharistic wedding feast: "Blessed are those who are invited to the marriage supper of the Lamb" (19:9), for they can gaze on the pure Bride of Christ, the heavenly city with its infinite wealth.

This biblical utopia is a utopia of controlled desires. The unconscious desires of the male reader are brought to the surface and redirected. Female desires for power are not allowed to continue. Females who desire power are monsters who drink men's blood, sleep with anyone who comes along, and give birth to whores and the "earth's abominations" (17:6). "A structure of feeling" (Newton/Rosenfelt 1985:10) is set up in the Apocalypse where the feelings of and feelings for women are under male domination. The Apocalypse means death to women—death to the affirmation of the female body and sexual desires and autonomy and erotic power. Real desire is decentered. The desire of women must be for a different utopia.

6

CONCLUSION: THE ENDLESS END OF THE WORLD

Confronting apocalypse, he exclaims with a horror close to ecstasy.

— Julia Kristeva, *Powers of Horror*

Presuppositions by which we approach the text affect how we read the text. Naming the ending of the Apocalypse as ending, as the concluding form of the narrative which brings closure, is a way of finding out what the text *means*. Rabinowitz (1987:161) notes, "Endings . . . are not always so neat, and when they are not, the reader is often expected to reinterpret the work so that the ending in fact serves as an appropriate conclusion."[1] Rabinowitz's discussion of the narrative conventions of textual endings recalls Lacan (1977:86): "The function of language is not to inform but to evoke." The evocative language of the Apocalypse leads to an infinite number of possible readings. In the end, the text betrays its own closure; the utopian vision is not enacted, and the angel pronounces that God's reign is just beyond reach:

> And he said to me, "Do not seal up the words of the prophecy of this book, for the time is near. Let the evildoer still do evil, and the filthy still be filthy, and the righteous still do right, and the holy still be holy." (22:10-11)

87

The new heaven and the new earth remain in the realm of desire. The world does not change, but God's activity on behalf of those who witness is outlined. The ending is disruptive, opening the ambiguity of the text to the reader, whose response cannot be predetermined. The reader participates in the endless end of the world every time the story is heard or read.

I am arguing that I see the Apocalypse in terms of plurality rather than unity. To borrow Annette Kolodny's phrase, there is a "playful pluralism" at work in the act of reading this biblical text. The desire for unity and cohesion is a natural one. To be honest, I too want to make sense of the Apocalypse—to examine every seam and stitch, and to trace the way the book is held together. I have desired so much for the theories of seven act dramas and chiasms to be definitive. I have desired clear connections between Emperor Domitian and the late first century CE world. But again I want to push against the boundaries of interpretation. I want to play with the theory that this text is an open text. I want to play with a deconstructive reading. Michael Harris (1989) explores a deconstructive reading of the Apocalypse:

> The insertion of the modifier "open" immediately calls to mind the concept of a "closed" poetics, or a poetics that is in some sort of conflict, or opposition, to an "open" (hence, pluralistic) poetics. One can certainly argue that an open poetics is not possible in any way. To place the term "open" in quotation marks is to come as close as possible at this time and in this context to placing it under erasure. . . . To interpret is thus to dance with the text, a dance that sometimes leads to blissful union, sometimes to death—the death of the critic and text (does the interpretation of the Apocalypse lead to bliss or death, or perhaps, blissful death?).

The desire for the center is what Derrida (1974) calls logocentrism, which includes the privileging of speech over writing (phonocentrism). Phonocentrism does not allow for différance, which involves the split between signifier and signified and for Derrida, the endless play between them. In the Apocalypse we find the privileging of speech over writing (phonocentrism) with the voices who speak to John and instruct him to write. But ultimately writing is privileged over speech: "Write this, for these words are trustworthy and true" (21:5). The threat of the curse of God exists, moreover, if one edits the written word (22:18-19). The "violent hierarchy" of speech/writing is overturned. In this way the text deconstructs itself.

A FANTASY OF THE END

I want to propose another way of referring to the Apocalypse. First of all, why do we use different terms for biblical and bible-related literature than we use for secular literature? Why not borrow the terms from those who specialize in literature and literary theory? In fact, secular "apocalypses" borrow from the biblical term.[2] One reason for our reluctance, no doubt, is that often the terms are foreign or threatening to biblical scholars. "Myth" was difficult enough to integrate into the biblical critic's vocabulary, and the term "fantasy" is only recently being introduced into the discussion. Fantasy is a different way of talking about apocalyptic literature. And I want to play with the idea that biblical apocalyptic literature is an early form of what we now call fantasy literature. The supernatural world of heroes and gods, mythic animals, and beasts, and epic battles in another realm reflects the fantastic.

As discussed earlier, one fantasy theorist/writer, Rosemary Jackson, describes fantasy in this way: "[It is] a literature of desire, which seeks that which is experienced as absence or loss" (1981:106). The reader is caught between the supernatural and the natural, and thus the reader's response (and often the response of characters in the story) is to hesitate. The cathartic effect of the Apocalypse is found in the moment of reading/hearing about and participating in the fantastic world where God liberates all the believers. Fantasy is the mode in which improbable events are probable, the "unreal" is "real," the abnormal is normal.

As I also pointed out earlier, Todorov's description of the categories of the fantastic includes: the fantastic-uncanny in which the supernatural is explained, and the fantastic-marvelous in which the supernatural is accepted by the reader and is not explained. One aspect of the fantastic-marvelous is horror literature (or dark fantasy), and I want to suggest that the Apocalypse also has elements of horror. In particular, the beasts/monsters of the Apocalypse invoke fear—what H. P. Lovecraft (1973) calls "cosmic fear." Horror theorist Noël Carroll (1990:145) observes,

> . . . many horror stories begin, so to speak, as fantastic narratives, but become horror as soon as the fact of the monster's existence is revealed to and acknowledged by the reader.

The descriptions of the monsters in the Apocalypse are drawn in vivid colors and with much detail. In chapter 12 the "great red dragon, with seven heads and ten horns, and seven diadems on his heads," is portrayed as the monster who wants to eat the messianic child as soon as it is born. The two beasts in chapter 13 are even more complicated in detail: the first beast has "ten horns and seven heads; and on its horns were ten diadems, and on its heads were blasphemous names. And the beast that I saw was like a leopard, its feet were like a bear's, and its mouth was like a lion's mouth" (13:1-2); the second beast "had two horns like a lamb and it spoke like a dragon" (13:11). When John sees the adorned Whore of Babylon he remarks, "When I saw her, I was greatly amazed" (17:6). These monsters are truly horrible and are drawn large to evoke fear and to push the reader toward decision.

But the good supernatural figures also evoke fear. The "one like the Son of Man" in 1:12-16 has flaming eyes and a "sharp, two-edged sword" coming out of his mouth. John's response: "When I saw him, I fell at his feet as though dead" (1:17). The angels with seals and trumpets and bowls of wrath who are messengers for the destruction, although they are not depicted in such grotesque terms, are nevertheless terrifying creatures. Carroll (1990:150) notes:

> For, on my view of horror, the supernatural or sci-fi monster whose existence is finally acknowledged must be fearsome and disgusting. But the fantastic-marvelous is equally satisfied whether the marvelous being is horrifying or not. For example, the marvelous being whose existence is finally acknowledged might be a benevolent angel.

The four living creatures and the angels in heaven are loud; for example in 10:2 the angel "gave a great shout, like a lion roaring. And when he shouted, the seven thunders sounded" (cf. 5:12; 7:2; 12:10; 14:15, 18; 16:1). The angels give strange instructions to John and serve as escorts through the visions. In one scene the seven angels with the plagues are described as "robed in pure bright linen, with golden sashes across their chests" (15:6). Even though these angels come from God and are doing God's work, they are nonetheless dangerous and provoke fear. They are given the power to destroy the earth and all its inhabitants, along with the evil powers.

This unveiling of the "truth" of the Apocalypse exposes the horror of the visions. The hoarse and heavy breathing in the distance or the subtle placing of the monster's hand on the victim's shoulder are not the techniques of this text. Instead, the monsters appear suddenly, in full and frightful form.

The supernatural realm in the narrative introduces some heart-stopping characters for both the character/narrator and the reader. The monsters are right before the reader, close enough to touch. The end of the Apocalypse points to the hope that God will defeat these evil powers. But for now, the monsters live.

The journey into the Apocalypse is a fantastic journey, with elements of triumph and joy and elements of horror and "cosmic fear." A range of desires is involved in the reading of the Apocalypse. Fantasy explores these desires and invites the reader to participate in the play of language and life.

The endless possibility for desire—the desire for death and the desire for erotic fulfillment—draws the reader deeper and deeper into the supernatural world as the text is read and reread. The Apocalypse is more than scary entertainment with a "happy ending" for the few. The cultural and religious imprint of this text has defiled desire as expressed in the erotic power of women. This world turned upside down dumps all the women out; the mothers of the revolution are excluded from the new order.

I have noted that as "resistance literature" the Apocalypse has an important message in certain oppressive political contexts. But can any misogynist text be truly liberating? Since this text is stuck so permanently and prominently in the biblical canon, I want to use it as a starting point for reading the whole canon in reverse, against itself, against the grain, and against the whole history of abuse of women. I am a resisting reader, desiring different visions, desiring difference, desiring the resistance that brings justice.

UTOPIAN DESIRE: THE DISCOURSE OF TOTALITY IN APOCALYPSE 21-22

At the end of the Apocalypse of John comes the resolution of the conflict. The desire for utopia, for a new heaven and new earth, is fulfilled.[3] The Apocalypse is about God's time—a time in which justice for the oppressed and judgment against the oppressors will not wait. But the reader must wait, and with patient introspection expect the reign of God and the creation of a just (but exclusive) new society.

Chapter 21 begins with the vision of the new heaven and new earth: "for the first heaven and the first earth had passed away, and the sea was no more." The chaos of the present world has passed, and God has come to live with humanity. In this New Jerusalem there is no suffering, pain, thirst, or death:

> See, the home of God is among mortals. He will dwell with them as their God; they will be his peoples, and God himself will be with them; he will wipe every tear from their eyes. Death will be no more; mourning and crying and pain will be no more, for the first things have passed away. And the one who was seated on the throne said, "See, I am making all things new." (21:3-5a)

This utopian world is not the rational world of Thomas More; rather, the emphasis is on the metaphorical.

In commenting on the thought of Hélène Cixous, Toril Moi (1985:121) suggests that "the utopian vision takes off from a negative analysis of its own society in order to create images and ideas that have the power to inspire to revolt against oppression and exploitation." She adds (1985:123) that utopias "challenge us both on the poetic and the political level."[4] The New Jerusalem, with all its jewels, gold, glass, and light, stands in direct contradiction to the destroyed Babylon. The new city "has the glory of God and a radiance like a very rare jewel, like jasper, clear as crystal" (21:11), and "people will bring into it the glory and the honor of the nations" (21:26).

The reader is reminded of the costs: only "those who conquer will inherit these things" (21:7; echoing the seven letters in chapters 2-3), along with those who wash their robes (22:14; 7:14). These are the insiders; the outsiders are comprised of "the murderers, the fornicators, the sorcerers, the idolaters, and all liars" (21:8) and "the dogs and sorcerers and fornicators and murders and idolaters, and everyone who loves and practices falsehood" (22:15). Their fate is sealed: "their place will be in the lake that burns with fire and sulphur, which is the second death" (21:8; 20:14). Again, there is "nothing unclean" in the New Jerusalem and "any one who practices abomination or falsehood" is not granted entrance (21:27).[5] The goal is achieved by God, but believers must take responsibility for their own choices.

Behind this utopian vision is the notion of desire. Northrop Frye (1957:157) states, "Apocalyptic symbolism presents the infinitely desirable, in which the lusts and ambitions of [humans] are identified with, adapted to, or projected on the gods."[6] The desire in the Apocalypse is two-fold: on the one hand there is the desire for violence against the oppressors (the Whore in Apoc 18 and the Devil in Apoc 20); on the other hand, there is the desire for a utopian society in which "nothing accursed will be found there any more" (22:3), and there will be no more violence or pain.

Michel Beaujour (1987:30) inserts a warning into the dual nature of this desire of violence and utopia, or in his words, "revolution and poetry." He says that "both are only promises: by making *present* what is beside and beyond, their absence is concealed" because they "try to wrap themselves in their utopias, without ever entirely succeeding." Beaujour is critical of revolutionary poetry for creating an "absent apocalypse," because "it procures for the mass a utopian dream, the flash of

catharsis, a holiday: it serves the authorities all too well!"
(1987:33). Such a negative view of the effects of utopian writing
fails to realize that the reader of such texts does not remain in
the utopian vision but steps out of time only briefly. This movement or step in and out of the utopian world does not mean
that the "real" world is suddenly forgotten. The possibility of
the beyond enters into the here and now.

How does the culmination of the utopian desire unfold in
chapters 21 and 22? Tobin Siebers' use (1984) of the feature of
suspense is helpful here. Although the reader must surely make
an ethical choice by choosing sides, these options are already
acted out in the narrative: the kings, merchants, and sailors
choose to dwell with the Whore, and the witnesses (martyrs)
choose to stand with God and the Lamb. The desire for the fall
of the oppressors and the salvation of the faithful creates great
suspense, and this suspense is only partially relieved in the
narrative. The characters' fate is sealed; but the fictional world
awaits the fulfillment of the prophecy: "Let the evildoer still do
evil, and the filthy still be filthy, and the righteous still do right,
and the holy still be holy" (22:10). The judgment on humanity
is still to come, but the guidelines are set. Siebers (1984:56)
discusses the aspect of suspense as caused by superstition:

> A crucial aspect of every fantastic story is the relation between
> the reader and the accused. If the reader decides to embrace
> the accused agent of the fantastic, the logic of superstition is
> allowed to endure. Expelling the accused serves to eliminate
> the supernatural.

According to Jackson (1981:3-4), desire is expressed in
different ways: the desire of the faithful for the coming of God's
realm and its benefits ("let anyone who wishes take the water of
life as a gift" [22:17]); and the desire that is expelled "when
this desire is a disturbing element which threatens cultural order
and continuity (expression in the sense of pressing out, squeez-
ing, expulsion, getting rid of something by force)." This rather
perverse desire to expel the oppressor (as well as the desire to
follow the oppressor), which is part of the desire for utopia,
leads the reader to the New Jerusalem. The impossibility becomes a possibility.

This gathering of God and the Lamb and all the servants with their washed robes has a sense of festivity. With all the light and jewels and the worship of the throne the scene in chapters 21-22 almost resembles Mikhail Bakhtin's concept (1973) of the carnival. Jackson (1981:16) makes this connection of carnival with the fantastic, since carnival, like fantasy, "was a temporary condition, a ritualized suspension of everyday law and order." Ernst Bloch also sees this aspect of utopia: "Art is at one and the same time a laboratory and a carnival of possibilities brought to fulfillment."[7] In the Apocalypse, however, there is a satirical reversal: those who had been part of the free-for-all carnival in the real world would not participate in the heavenly "carnival." There is a certain raw abandonment of the status quo that is called for earlier in the narrative. In these last chapters the choices have been made; the utopian festival has begun.

With the "real" world subverted and the joys of the utopian society experienced, the reader returns to the "safe" world. In his study of lethic reading Clayton Koelb (1984:227) notes that "disbelief protects the reader . . . keeping the dangerous power of liberated speech away from the reader." So are we to believe this fantastic story of the New Jerusalem and the fulfillment of prophecy of the Apocalypse? Or have we been sucked in by one big lie? The dream of utopian totality remains a dream— remains in absence/presence in the narrative, even though it is God who tells the narrator, "Write this, for these words are trustworthy and true" (21:5; 22:6). Other voices are heard— heavenly voices of authority—but the liberated society which was envisioned has not occurred. Christianity's eventual merger with the state did not change the systems of taxation and totalitarian rule or create the realm of God on earth.

So what went wrong? Is the apocalyptic fantasy only a quick, confusing trip into the "beyond"—a brief encounter with the Other? Such questions of truth and falsity are better understood in terms of "a rhetoric of the unreal" (Brooke-Rose 1981). Fantasy literature does not claim to mirror reality directly; rather it illuminates the real world. The fictional nature of the fantastic destabilizes the rational world. Its rhetoric is unreal, not

providing escape, but allowing silent voices to speak and unconscious desires to be enacted.

Robert Scholes offers a way of understanding this dialogical
relationship between the Apocalypse and the real. In examining
science fiction texts Scholes found similarities with the romantic,
or fabulation "that offers us a world clearly and radically
discontinuous from the one we know, yet returns to confront
that known world in some cognitive way" (Scholes 1975:29).
He divides fabulation into dogmatic (religious) and speculative
fabulation (science fiction). The Apocalypse fits into the category of dogmatic speculation, since the prophecies are clearly
expected/desired to "occur" in the near future (22:6; 1:1).

If Scholes is correct about the confrontation that occurs with
the "known world" both during and after the reading of fantastic literature, the desire for the institution of the utopian world
is politically dangerous. To imagine the confrontation of good
and evil (oppressed and oppressor) and the defeat of the enemy
is a powerful experience. The imagination is allowed to play
freely within the boundaries of the fantastic vision. Anxiety is
both raised and settled. The fantastic journey carries us to the
edge of culture and the edge of politics and the edge of ideology. Foundations are shaken, cultural norms are questioned, and
the dominant ideology is ruptured. Studies in the fantastic
enable us to read that boundless future. The Apocalypse of
John is about the revolutionary event of the creation of God's
utopia. It is about the incarnation of hope and of the coming of
the Alpha and the Omega. But the completion of God's utopia
remains unfinished. And the "holy war" continually returns.

WOMEN AND WAR:
THE REPRODUCTION OF POWER

The ideology of gender in the Apocalypse is not only linked to
the biological sphere of giving birth or eating and drinking or
fornicating or remaining a virgin. Reading for gender in the text
reveals the nature of the cultural and political predicament of
women, and exposes the dominant male attitudes for what they
really are. The holy war of God, the Lamb, and company pits
heavenly army against man and demon figures, man against

man, and man against woman. Ultimately, the "death-dealing binary oppositions" (Hélène Cixous) are set up between male and female. The women in the struggle (Jezebel, the Woman Clothed with the Sun, and the Whore) are all victims of the war. On the political level there is the horror of the war, with its massive natural disasters and bloodshed, for the martyrs and for the enemies of the Lamb. But the horror of the war in this text is for women the ultimate horror, and the heavenly Bride is the only female left to celebrate the victory.

The discourse of war is inscribed in the text. The believers are to remain creatively nonviolent, even to the point of death. God is in control of the violent revolution. Lacan notes: "It is the irony of revolutions that they engender a power all the more absolute in its actions, not because it is more anonymous, as people say, but because it is more reduced to the words which signify it" (in Hassan 1984:441).

The ideology of the revolution is based on the opposition of the powers of God with the powers of evil. The either-or ethic of the Apocalypse (the choice for either Christ or Satan) is played on the open forum of desires. The desire for the wealth and lifestyle which are signified in the Whore is played out to the bitter end. Those who conquer this desire are rewarded (2:7, 11, 17; 3:5, 12, 21) with eternal life, heavenly food, clothes, a place of honor in the heavenly temple near the throne of God. Those who conquer are also granted "power over the nations" (2:26), to which I would add, power over women.

The desire for earthly power is seen as the desire for an erotically powerful woman. This power is evil and corrupt and is built at the expense of the lives of the martyrs. The wish of the oppressed is the revolution which overthrows the oppressor and puts the oppressed in power. But in the Apocalypse the war has a different purpose—one of affirming and concretizing God's power and eternal rule.

The desire for death, the desire for desire, the death of female desire and the fulfillment of male desire—all of these aspects enter into a discussion of the ideology of gender in the text. Alice Jardine's description of ideology (1986:85) is suggestive: "I would insist upon ideology as the conceptual glue of culture, that which makes culture seem natural, that which holds any cultural system together, that which, in fact, makes any system of relationships appear natural." The ideology of the dominant power is deprivileged and eventually eliminated in the Apocalypse; whereas the ideology of gender is revalorized. Women are symbolized in male terms. Those who loved the Whore suddenly hate her (17:16). The male decides the fate of all the women in the Apocalypse.

I have been taught how to read war—to root for violence. So I used to root for the forces of God who overthrow the Whore in the Apocalypse. Nonviolence is the way of gylany, the way of women's relationships in the world. Power is reproduced in the narrative but not in women's terms. Desire is a powerful force in the text; if you desire God it may cost you your life at the hands of the dominant power.

But the ideology of the Apocalypse is not as simple and straightforward as I once thought. As Newton and Rosenfelt (1985:xix) discover, "Ideology is a system of representations through which we experience *ourselves* as well, for the work of ideology is also to construct coherent subjects." This definition is certainly Althusserian—but with a twist. The twist is the affirmation of gender differences in the study of ideology: the emphasis on woman as subject, the material realities, and the cultural base of knowledge. As Susan Griffin (1981:257) states, "True eros reflects the whole of human experience. . . . Desire and meaning are not separate." Women are set up in the Apocalypse as the opposite of men—as other and separate. Utopia is not whole, but rather maintains this separation and hierarchy of power. The transformation of society in the Apocalypse is only partial transformation.

The Apocalypse describes the final eschatological battle in all its extreme violence and gory detail. There is a certain catharsis to this holy war. This war is "the war to end all wars." God's army conquers the evil powers. Both men and women are subject to death by this army. This holy war is by no means a "just war," mainly because civilian noncombatants are targeted. The believers who are called to "patient endurance"

98

must resist nonviolently, but this resistance is active, not passive, since the result of being a witness (read "martyr") might be death. What are women's roles in this war? How are contemporary women readers to respond to God's war?

The violence and vengeance in the Apocalypse come out of the experience of persecution: "I, John, your brother who share with you in Jesus the persecution and the kingdom and the patient endurance" (1:9). The violence of the book is startling; violence is done to nature and people and supernatural beings. There are swords and slaughter and hunger and martyrs. The people of all classes who hide in the cave say to the mountain: "Fall on us and hide us from the face of the one seated on the throne and from the wrath of the Lamb; for the great day of their wrath has come, and who is able to stand?" (Apoc 6:16-17). The wrath of God and the Lamb is so great that people cannot "face" them.

The war is bloody; there are casualties on both sides. Cannibalism is part of the warfare tactics—the kings and merchants eat the Whore and are in turn eaten by the birds of midheaven, who "gather for the great supper of God" (Apoc 19:17). There is torture in the lake of fire and sulfur (Apoc 20:10): "This is the second death, the lake of fire; and anyone whose name was not found written in the book of life was thrown into the lake of fire" (Apoc 20:15). All the enemies and every impure thing (the old earth, especially the sea) is destroyed (21:1). The New Jerusalem comes down to replace the old city: "Come, I will show you the bride, the wife of the Lamb." And in the spirit he carried me away to a great, high mountain and showed me the holy city Jerusalem coming down out of heaven from God" (21:9-10). There is no evil or pollution in the new world. The new world of God far surpasses the old world.

The description of the final battle is fantastic. The rider of the white horse "is called Faithful and True, and in righteousness he judges and makes war" (19:11); "he is clothed in a robe dipped in blood, and his name is called The Word of God" (19:13); "on his robe and on his thigh he has a name inscribed, 'King of kings and Lord of lords'" (19:16). The armies of this leader follow on white horses, wearing white linen (19:14). The symbolic universe of a supernatural battle involves the imagination of the reader. This narrative does call for a nonviolent ethical stance; God's heavenly army will do all the "dirty work." The rider on the white horse strikes down the rulers and nations with the sword of his mouth (19:15a, 21); "he will tread the wine press of the fury of the wrath of God the Almighty" (19:15b). But the imagination is endless, and the connection between the desire of the reader and the desire in the text has endless possibilities.

The fantasy of the end time has mimetic potential. Again, Rosemary Jackson's definition of fantasy relates the political with the textual: ". . . fantasies image the possibility of radical cultural transformation through attempting to dissolve or shatter the boundary lines between the imaginary and the symbolic" (1981:178). Fantasy literature is not escapist; rather, fantasy exposes the reader to what is "real" through the symbols of the supernatural and the magical. The violence and vengeance that is part of this fantasy world in the Apocalypse exposes the violence in the "real" world. But also exposed is the desire for the violent destruction of the enemy at the hands of God.

Is this desire for violence part of women's ways of knowing? Or is this desire the patriarchal image/imagining of the end? Do women desire a violent apocalypse? Literal interpretations of the Apocalypse get caught up in the violent details. Jean Elshtain (1987:247) points to the effect of these fundamentalist readings: "Apocalyptic warnings may be balm to the spirit of many, rather than a way to strike terror and in so doing to promote action." The bonds of such a passive response to the Apocalypse have to be broken.

Alice Walker responds bluntly and honestly to "the hope for revenge" against the enemies: "*Let the earth marinate in poisons. Let the bombs cover the ground like rain. For nothing short of total destruction will ever teach them anything*" (1982: 264). Then Walker points to a different knowledge, a different response:

So let me tell you: I intend to protect my home. Praying—not a curse—only the hope that my courage will not fail my love.

But if by some miracle, and all our struggle, the earth is spared, only justice to every living thing (and everything is alive) will save humankind. And we are not saved yet. *Only justice can stop a curse.* (1982:265)

The survivalist ethic of women of color turns curse into courage. Women set the terms of salvation, not the male God on his distant throne.

Walker speaks the account of her vision like Sojourner Truth, with a voice like "apocalyptic thunders" (see Eugene: 28). Walker is able to face the nuclear apocalypse brought about by the white males in power. She shakes us out of our sleep. As Jonathan Schell warns, "We drowse our way toward the end of the world" (1982:239). It takes voices of "apocalyptic thunders" to wake us.

Part of facing apocalypse is learning to "sustain the gaze." This phrase from Joanna Macy means a breaking free of our denial of the nuclear apocalypse. As a concrete example of what women are doing to "sustain the gaze," Macy includes the women protesters of cruise missiles at Greenham Common. She calls their action "apocalyptic or "uncovering" behavior" (1987:167). In the late twentieth century women are called to active resistance—to take part in facing the end.

As Catherine Keller recognizes, "The nuclear complex must be faced and healed if it is not to bring on the end of time" (1990:77). Helen Cauldicott, the women of Women's Action for New Directions (formerly, Women's Action for Nuclear Disarmament), Physicians for Social Responsibility, the women speaking in the documentary, "Women for America, For the World," and Sane/Freeze are all speaking of the doom to allow us to break out of our denial.

The holy war of the Apocalypse is no longer an option. As Schell reveals, "The choices don't include war any longer. They consist now of peace, on the one hand, and annihilation, on the other" (1982:193). Women's response to the coming apocalypse has to be a reinterpretation of what it means to choose Christ over Satan. Choosing Christ no longer means desiring martyrdom. When two-thirds of the earth's population goes to bed hungry each night, martyrdom becomes another form of patriarchal abuse. Christ is more than a sacrificial lamb who resurrected into a mythic warrior hero. Women have to refuse the call to mimic such sacrifice. Women (and men!) must be involved in risk-taking for social change.[8]

War always involves a dialectic of yes and no. And women have said both yes and no to war. In an article entitled, "Tales of War and Tears of Women," Nancy Huston argues that the telling or narrative of a war is necessary for its "reality." She shows how women play "supporting roles" in the war perfor- mance: as pretext, booty, recompense, casualties, miracle mothers and castrating bitches, and cooperative citizens, to name a few roles (1982:275). Of women who say no to war Huston elaborates on an example of women who laughed instead of wept at military power: "These women said no, they laughed in the face of the ineluctable, they refused to collabo- rate in the making of tragedy, they denounced it for what it is: a theatre of the absurd" (1982:282). Is all war, even holy war, "theatre of the absurd"? I think women's (and men's) response is to laugh and say, yes.

The Apocalypse ends after the war, after the destruction of the old earth. A utopia ("no place") is set up by God. "Death will be no more; mourning and crying and pain will be no more, for the first things have passed away" (Apoc 21:4). God and the Lamb dwell inside the city with the chosen people. The new world is perfectly pure, and there is no more suffering. Is this male fantasy of a utopia of limited diversity and the war to make it happen what women want? For women who say no to supporting roles in this holy war, what is the alternative apoca- lyptic narrative? Do we really want to accept the ideology of the Apocalypse? Do we seek this utopian idea/l? Does reading the Apocalypse as a woman mean desiring a different ending? The apocalypse of women has always included the horrors of war. What does it mean for women to read the ultimate war narra- tive? Is this violent version of the end of time the story women want to tell—the story women want to be involved in? The New Jerusalem is tragic. Women do not rejoice. Women do not desire this utopia brought about by famine and war and pesti- lence and natural disaster. I can hear the objections of my male friends, "But we don't desire that either!" Yet the place of the Apocalypse in the canon remains an immutable part of Christian history.

A UTOPIA FOR WOMEN?

The utopian political fantasy is directly related to communal human experience as a liberating, cathartic, revolutionary, symbolic experience. Liberation (materialist) readings of texts have always warned against such emphasis on the general (here, the cosmic), because oppression and marginalization are always specific, always personal. The female figures in the Apocalypse are given symbolic names and symbolic tasks; they are not allowed to speak their own identity. This technique distances the reader from the female images, leaving only women stereotypes of good and evil and no real flesh and blood women. But then the Apocalypse is about a symbolic universe, and is a parody of flesh and blood reality. The female images are part of the larger paradigm of the final scenes in the liberation of the oppressed.

Yet this explanation is distorted in the narrative. In the Christian utopia, expectations of power and authority are reversed—the Beast is defeated and the Lamb rules. At least the expectations for *men* are reversed; women are left exactly where they were in Mediterranean society—excluded from the realm of power. The utopia ("no place") for men is an atopia ("not a place") for women. The marriage of the Bride and the Lamb brings hope (brings utopia), but is not an inclusive model for women. Women have historically been excluded from many areas of culture, but are they also excluded in this text from the New Jerusalem? What happens to the female believers other than being subsumed under this image of the Bride? Here the text is silent.

In their anthropological study of female roles in culture, Judith Hoch-Smith and Anita Spring summarize the mythical representation of the female images: "The idea of female evil is transformed into specific cultural expression through *the manifestation of that culture's ideological content in art* . . . Female sexuality is seen as a disruptive, chaotic force that must be controlled or coopted by men, periodically purified, and at times destroyed'' (1978:3; emphasis mine). The ideology of the female in the Apocalypse remains true to the dominant ideology of its culture.

But when women read the narrative (especially contemporary women readers), the experience is like that delineated by Jonathan Culler (1982:44): "When we posit a woman reader, the result is an analogous appeal to experience: not to the experience of girl-watching but to the experience of being watched, seen as a "girl," restricted, marginalized." Women readers of the Apocalypse are typed, hunted, adorned, and rejected. The domination of male over female remains intact.

Jameson (1981:290) is correct on one level (that of the class struggle in History) when he points to the relationship of utopia and ideology: "ideological commitment is not first and foremost a matter of moral choice but of the taking of sides in a struggle between embattled groups . . . [and] must always necessarily be focused on the class enemy." On the level of gender differences and conflict, however, Jameson's analysis falls short. Ideology is also gender based and biased. The Apocalypse focuses on the class enemy but neglects the oppressed/oppressor categories of gender relations. In the political realm women are defeated or banished to the wilderness; only the submissive, sexual Bride is allowed at the utopian feast of the Lamb. The image and the function of the female remains ambiguous: the erotic desire of the narrative remains intact with the symbol of the Bride, but the men who enter her must be ritually pure, and the female figures with any sexual autonomy (the Jezebel, the Whore, and the Woman Clothed with the Sun share this feature) are pushed out or to the edge.

If the writer of the Apocalypse is treated to the same gender critique as writers like Paul, Chaucer, and Rabelais, there will probably emerge defenders on both sides: those who defend the writer, "John," as "a man of his era" in which women were debased and powerless, and those who accuse and dismiss the writer as continuing sexist ideology which is of no use to women. A feminist reading can focus on the remnants of goddesses reflected in the winged flight of the Woman Clothed with the

Sun and the murder of the Whore. Or a feminist reading can hope with Roland Barthes (1972:57) that the future will involve a destruction of the past "in which the potent seed of the future *is nothing but* the most profound apocalypse of the present."

The destruction of the past means the destruction of *all* the forces of oppression. The Christian Apocalypse of John, however, is limited in its destruction. The irony of the grotesque burning of the Whore is that the Christian utopia is itself an oppressive world (for women). In other words, for women there is no escaping oppression (except to flee to the wilderness?). Historically, the church eventually merges with the Roman state. And Christian women seek autonomy in the monastery (in the wilderness) in a sexually exclusive environment. But in the Apocalypse narrative, gender oppression is left untouched by the sword of God.

The tale of the Apocalypse is not a tale of the liberation of female consciousness. The Apocalypse is not a tale for women. The misogyny which underlies this narrative is extreme. Women of the past as well as the present are going to have to be about the business of creating their own apocalyptic tales, their own utopian narratives.

REWRITING THE APOCALYPSE FOR WOMEN

I have been reading some feminist utopian literature lately, from Ursula LeGuin's *The Dispossessed* to more overtly feminist utopias such as Charlotte Perkins Gilman's *Herland*, Joanna Russ' *The Female Man*, and Marge Piercy's *Woman on the Edge of Time*. In comparing these utopian texts to the Apocalypse, I am struck by their female (in most cases only female) futures. An agrarian world without war, a world where technology allows women to procreate without men, a world without gender strife—these are all common themes in feminist science fiction.

When these 19th- and 20th-century women imagine the future, it is drastically different from the vision of the seer John on the island of Patmos. If these books were arranged in a bookstore, one would find all the women writers under "science fiction." The Apocalypse, on the other hand, would be found under "horror literature."

But is this a fair comparison? Is it not in the "nature" of apocalypses to be about violent destruction and violent imposition of a new order? In the Apocalypse of John is there not an oppressive colonial political situation to be addressed that takes precedence over other concerns? Well, yes, maybe, but Gayatri Spivak (1983:185) makes a good point about feminist criticism rewriting "the social text so that the historical and sexual differentials are operated together."

The apocalyptic future, the utopia of the Apocalypse is individualistic. There is competition for power and control—but most of all for place, a place, in the book of life and in the heavenly place. Charlotte Perkins Gilman imagined a different place in 1915 during World War I. She envisioned a women's utopia on this earth where there was no competition or war. One of the three men who discovered this utopian community comments:

> As I learned more and more to appreciate what these women had accomplished, the less proud I was of what we, with all our manhood, had done. You see, they had no wars. They had no kings, and no priests, and no aristocracies. They were sisters, and as they grew, they grew together—not by competition, but by united action. (1979:60)

Gilman's vision is certainly idealistic, and she has been cited for her elitism and racism, which has to be noted as we dream about the next millennium. But the dream of "united action," a global action, pushes women toward the future. Women will testify to a different apocalyptic vision, a different utopia.

The future for women is part of the subtext of the Apocalypse. Women are to mimic the roles of the "good" archetypes of mother of the messiah and Bride. The future for women is to become like the Bride, adorned for her husband and submissive to his wishes. Woman as city (Babylon or the New Jerusalem) lays herself out as sacrifice. Like the goddess Tiamat whose body is used to form the earth, the Bride becomes the heavenly city and God's church. But unlike the Tiamat story, there is no fight.

The Bride and the Woman Clothed with the Sun are kept safe from the war. There is even a wedding feast in the midst of the fighting (Apoc 19:9). The Brussels Tapestry of the marriage of the Lamb (mid-sixteenth century) shows the festivities of the marriage supper, with a beautiful, smiling Bride with her arm around the Lamb. The guests around the table are worshiping the Lamb. But directly above the Bride's head lies the burning Whore, surrounded by flames with a look of horror on her face and a eucharistic-type cup in her hand. The juxtaposition of these two scenes is disturbing. Is the burning of the Whore the desire of women? Are we to identify with the smiling Bride as "ideal woman"?

I am not out to demythologize apocalyptic literature. I want to enter boldly into these mythical and fictional worlds—these fantastic landscapes—and see what there is to see. I want to encounter face to face the beasts and dragons and the Lamb and the heavenly angels. I want to encounter face to face the exiled and battered women. Here lies the call of the Apocalypse for women readers: to face the divisions of women by the patriarchy and to face our own roles in the violence. This facing is no easy task; the images in the Apocalypse are grotesque, and my reaction is to turn away from the violence—to seek some other text.

"Sustaining the gaze" at the Apocalypse is important for women readers because the gaze is necessary for breaking through denial over the apocalypse of women. Gazing at the biblical apocalypse enables women to gaze at the contemporary apocalypse. The parousia, the coming of Christ, will not be brought about by the further sacrifice and martyrdom of women (or men). The Apocalypse leaves women with no option for the future; the future is predetermined by God. But at the turn of the millennium women do have choices. Women in the Apocalypse are silenced, but women readers today have voices to speak to, of and about the biblical and contemporary apocalypses. We need to develop voices of "apocalyptic thunders."

NOTES

BIBLIOGRAPHY

INDEXES

ILLUSTRATIONS

NOTES

NOTES TO CHAPTER 1:
INTRODUCTION

[1] I am using the definition of reader from Pauline Marie Rosenau: "Reader—observer. Post-modernism is reader-oriented and gives readers the power of interpreting a text that, in modern terms, belonged to the author. Post-modern readers are dramatically empowered" (1992:xiii).

[2] The most comprehensive study of catharsis is by Adnan K. Abdulla (1985). Abdulla follows Ernst Cassirer in understanding catharsis not in terms of purgation but in terms of "a change in the human soul" when the soul is brought to peace after a cathartic experience (5-6).

[3] Here Abdulla packs in the understandings of Aristotle, Freud, Cassirer, Nietzsche, Hegel, Lukács, and drama theorists. Catharsis is clarification for Leon Golden (1969) as well, who sees in catharsis reader identification.

[4] See also Burke (1963).

[5] In one piece of medieval art in the Bodleian Library at Oxford some of the elect are lambs surrounding the Lamb. See Frederick van der Meer (1978:165).

[6] See Eagleton (1976:78-79): "In formalist terms the signifying practice is dominant over the signified creating "defamiliarisation.""

[7] See Foucault's notion (1977) of the "political technology of the body." See also Jameson (1981:90). Jacques Ellul (1977:94) proposes that the "state is not only force and power but also seduction and the captivity to make itself adored," and on page 98 adds, "What political power uses propaganda to bring about unanimity, to inspire adoration, to produce loyalty with fault?"

[8] Jacques Derrida (1987:285): "If death is not opposable it is, already, *life death.*"

[9] Good surveys of desire are found in Sam Girgus (1990); Eugene Goodheart (1991); Patricia Meyer Spacks (1990); Julia Kristeva (1980); Antoine Vergote (1988); René Girard (1965); Neal Oxenhandler (1988); Judith Butler (1987); Roland Barthes (1975); Marilyn Brown-

stein (1985); Sarah Spence (1988); Jean Wyatt (1990); Evelyn Vitz (1989).

[10] On p. 264, Bataille adds, "Eroticism is silence, I have said; it is solitude."

NOTES TO CHAPTER 2:
THE POLITICS OF THE END OF THE WORLD

[1] See Gregory Linton (1991).

[2] For example, the letters in Apoc 2-3 are letters from God—postcards in the Derridean sense. See Stephen Moore's (1992) reading of Mark as postcard.

[3] See Barbara Harlow (1987:2): "The term "resistance" . . . proposes an important distinction between literature which has been written "under occupation" . . . and "exile" . . . literature. Such a distinction presupposes a people's collective relationship to a common land, a common identity, or a common cause on the basis of which it becomes possible to articulate the difference between the two modes of historical and political existence, between, that is, "occupation" and "exile." Literature, in other words, is presented by the critic as an arena of *struggle*."

[4] Emile Benveniste (1971:43-48) corrects Saussure and says that signification and not the relationship between signifier and signified is arbitrary. Signifier and signified "make up the ensemble as the embodier and the embodied" (45).

[5] Jameson (1981:35). Absent cause—Spinoza; Real—Lacan. Also important is the description of Jameson's method by John Frow (1986:31-41). Terry Eagleton (1975:72) states: "It is rather that history is "present" in the text in the form of a double-absence."

[6] Gayatri Spivak (1987:122) discusses this quote. Martin Jay expresses a similar idea when he says that "a true utopianism understands that the future is latent in uncompleted remnants of the past as well as in the cutting edge of the present" (1984:189).

[7] "Trace" is a Derridean term. According to Eagleton, "The political task of "liberating" an object, then, takes the form of opening up its unconscious—detecting within it those chips of heterogeneity that it has been unable quite to dissolve" (1981:53). See Frow (1986: 42), for more on this quotation. On a more pragmatic level, Elie Wiesel has raised the same concerns in his writings on the Jewish Holocaust. For years he repressed his feelings about his youth in Nazi concentration camps and the deaths there of his parents and sister. Later he pushed for the importance of remembering these events and retelling

the horror to conscienticize future generations so that anti-Semitism will end and there will never be another Auschwitz in human history. Compare Foucault's concept of "dangerous memory."

8 Dowling (1984:188) explains Jameson: "It is the nightmare of history itself as men and women have always lived it, a nightmare that must be repressed as a condition of psychological survival not only by the master but also by the slave, not only by the bourgeoisie but also by the proletariat."

9 See Jameson (1981:53-54). Jameson uses Joseph Conrad's *Lord Jim* as an example of strategies of containment (210-219; 266-270).

10 Jameson (1981:31) sets up his hierarchy of the four levels of reading as follows: anagogical (political); moral (psychological); allegorical ("allegorical key or interpretive code"); literal ("historical or textual referent").

11 The idea of horizon is from Hans-Georg Gadamer (1975:216-220; 267-274). See Jameson (1981:75-76). See also the discussion horizons in Clarence Walhout (1986:137-139) and Dowling (1984:127-142).

12 The basic idea of transcendent interpretation is from Gilles Deleuze and Felix Guattari's idea of "immanent criteria" and the schizophrenic text (1977:25-28; 109-113; 305-308).

13 See Jameson (1981:67): "Even if the theory of desire is a metaphysic and a myth, it is one whose great narrative events—*repression and revolt*—ought to be congenial to Marxist perspective" (emphasis mine). On desire see also Jameson (1991:202-203).

14 Jameson (1971::84). West notes that the notion of freedom serves as the "center" (1983:181).

15 Eagleton further states (1983:210): "Indeed "ideology" can be taken to indicate no more than this connection—the link or nexus between discourses and power." See also Eagleton's excellent introduction to ideology (1991).

16 Bloch focused on the issue of art and utopia in many essays, which have been gathered together (Bloch 1988). Especially interesting are the articles from 1959: "The Conscious and Known Activity within the Not-Yet-Conscious, the Utopian" and "The Artistic Illusion as the Visible Anticipatory Illumination." In the latter Bloch states, *"The concrete utopia stands at the horizon of every reality; the real possibility encloses the open dialectical tendency-latency until the very last moment"* (155). Bloch is referring to Aristotle's "unfinished entelechy."

17 M. H. Abrams (1971:334) relates apocalyptic literature to

revelation, revolution, imagination, and cognition: "Faith in an apocalypse by revelation has been replaced by faith in an apocalypse by revolution, and this now gave way to faith in an apocalypse by imagination or cognition."

[18] Concerning the broader subject of the supernatural, Todorov (1973:82) states, "If the fantastic constantly makes use of rhetorical figures, it is because it originates in them. The supernatural is born of language, it is both its consequence and its proof."

[19] Gary K. Wolfe (1982:13) lists the structure of fantasy literature in the following points: cognition of the impossible; location of the impossible; delimitation of the impossible; feeling of the impossible; awareness of affective significance; awareness of cognitive significance, or deeper meaning; belief; deeper belief. He says that fantasies which lead the reader to deeper belief are rare. I think the Apocalypse accomplishes this level.

[20] See Jameson (1981); Zipes (1986:176); Jules Zanger (1982: 227); and Eric Rabkin (1976:12; 42).

NOTES TO CHAPTER 3:
AN APOCALYPSE OF WOMEN

[1] The speaker is "Glynnis Mullis, 27, homemaker and member of charismatic church, St. Simons Island." From *The Atlanta Journal and Constitution*, 15 January 1991.

[2] On the use of the term "third world," see Chandra Talpade Mohanty (1991).

[3] Filmmaker and critic Trinh T. Minh-ha comments on the relationship of insider and outsider: ". . . where should the line between insider and outsider stop? How should it be defined? By skin color, by language, by geography, by nation or by political affinity? What about those, for example, with hyphenated identities and hybrid realities?" (1990:374).

NOTES TO CHAPTER 5:
FANTASY AND THE FEMALE

[1] A similar placing of the land as an object of desire is done by Girgus (1990:9-10) in his study of the land of America in American literature: "Many Europeans thought of America in terms of love, sexuality and womanhood. Note how John Donne's nineteenth elegy exploits and perpetuates the comparison between America and a woman of love and mystery who promises a new paradise of freedom . . . This notion of America that relates her geography to the innermost

needs and wishes of human experience developed concomitantly with the basic values and beliefs that came to establish the American ideology of consensus." See also Kolodny (1975).

[2] Judith Hoch-Smith and Anita Spring (1978:2) provide a brief summary of "chaotic female sexuality." They state emphatically: "In no religious system do women's dominant metaphors derive from characteristics other than their sexual and reproductive status . . . Women are strikingly one-dimensional characters in mythology and ritual action. Images of women are reduced to their sexual function, women are excluded from leadership roles in most public rituals, and images of the divine are usually male."

[3] See Spivak's discussion on Derrida on orgasm as crime (1983:175).

[4] Marie Maclean (1987:45).

[5] Bottingheimer (1987:78) adds, "In *Grimms' Tales*, however, silence is almost exclusively female; enforced silence exists for both heroines and heroes as a precondition for redeeming oneself or others; and it also exists as a punishment for heroines (but not heroes) and as a narrative necessity for heroines (but not heroes) as in "The Robber-Bridegroom". In another article (1986:130) Bottigheimer states that "one must conclude that fairy tales offered an apparently innocent and peculiarly suitable medium for both transmitting and enforcing the norm of the silent woman . . . serving as paradigms for powerlessness."

[6] Marcia Landy (1977:27) summarizes the problem: "for the most part women have concurred, have accepted the male images as their own or have created accommodations satisfactory to them within the given power structure—a Virgin Queen, an Amazon, a Wielder of Power over Children and Lovesick Men—or women have agreed to see themselves as witches, demons, and deceivers. The consequences of straying from legitimized social norms were obviously too costly to entertain—deprivation of God, of man, of sociability, of economic sustenance, of biological needs."

[7] See Elizabeth Grosz (1989:149f).

NOTES TO CHAPTER 6:
CONCLUSION

[1] See Rabinowitz (1987:158-169): "Rules of Naming, Bundling, and Thematizing."

[2] One example is Morton Bloomfield (1961).

[3] Elisabeth Schüssler Fiorenza (1985:52) divides this eschato-

logical section into two parts: 21:1-8 (new Jerusalem) and 21:9-22:5 ("paradise tradition"). She notes the connection between the letters and these last visions—both include parenesis and visions. Christine Brooke-Rose (1981:ch. 9) offers an interesting narratological reading of fantasy and in particular of Tolkein. She uses such categories as "the plethora of information," readability (semiological compensation), and a whole complex system, which I think would be useful to future study on the Apocalypse.

4 Moi (1985:22) notes that the importance of Cixous' writings on utopia lies in her emphasis on "a flight from the dominant social reality." Moi relates that for Cixous "utopian thought . . . struggles to free itself from that patriarchal stranglehold."

5 Schüssler Fiorenza (1991:113-114) relates: "God's ideal city is not only a universal and inclusive city with a population drawn from all nations, but it is also magnificent and beautiful . . . Although there are still "insiders and outsiders," the gates of God's city are permanently open." The New Jerusalem is an "open inclusive place of citizenship and well-being for all."

6 Katherine Hume (1984:55-57) says that the literature of vision "invites us to experience a new sense of reality, a new interpretation that often seems more varied and intense than our own. Instead of turning our backs on everyday reality, as we do when seeking illusion, we absorb a new vision." The aim of vision is to disturb, and its effect is to engage. The literature of revision "like the literature of vision . . . strives to engage us, but unlike it, the aim is not so much to disturb us as to offer the eventual comfort of order, of a program, of decisions made and rules laid down. It offers us the emotional pleasures of absolutes."

7 Quoted in Jameson (1971:150).

8 On risk-taking, see Sharon Welch (1990).

BIBLIOGRAPHY

Abdulla, Adnan K. 1985. *Catharsis in Literature*. Bloomington: Indiana Univ.

Abrams, M. H. 1971. *Natural Supernaturalism: Tradition and Revolution in Romantic Literature*. New York: W. W. Norton.

Anzaldúa, Gloria. 1981. "La Pieta." In *This Bridge Called My Back: Writings by Radical Women of Color*. Eds. Cherrie Moraga and Gloria Anzaldúa. Pp. 198-209. New York: Kitchen Table/Women of Color.

———. 1987. *Borderlands/La Frontera*. San Francisco: Spinsters/Aunt Lute.

———. 1990. "Haciendo caras, una entrada." In *Making Face, Making Soul=Haciendo Caras: Creative and Critical Perspectives by Women of Color*. Ed. Gloria Anzaldúa. Pp. xv-xxviii. San Francisco: Aunt Lute Foundation.

Alexiou, Margaret. 1974. *The Ritual Lament in Greek Tradition*. Cambridge: Cambridge Univ.

Allen, V. and T. Paul. 1986. "Science and Fiction: Ways of Theorizing about Women." In *Erotic Universe: Sexuality and Fantastic Literature*. Ed. Donald Palumbo. Pp. 165-183. New York: Greenwood.

Alter, Robert. 1989. *The Pleasures of Reading in an Ideological Age*. New York: Simon and Schuster.

Apter, T. E. 1982. *Fantasy Literature: An Approach to Reality*. Bloomington: Indiana Univ.

Bakhtin, Mikhail. 1984. *Problems of Dostoevsky's Poetics*. Ed. and trans. Caryl Emerson. Minneapolis: Univ. of Minnesota.

Barr, David. 1990. "The 'Reader' of/in the Apocalypse: The Audience in Light of Reader Response Theory." Unpublished manuscript.

Barr, Marleen. 1975. *Future Females: A Critical Anthology*. Bowling Green: Bowling Green State Univ.

Barthes, Roland. 1972. *Mythologies*. Trans. Annette Lavers. New York: Hill and Wang.

———. 1974. *S/Z*. Trans. R. Miller. London: Jonathan Cape.

———. 1975. *The Pleasure of the Text*. Trans. Richard Miller. New York: Hill and Wang.

———. 1986. *The Rustle of Language*. Trans. Richard Howard. New York: Hill and Wang.

Bartkowski, Frances. 1987-1988. "A Fearful Fancy: Some Reconsiderations of the Sublime." *Boundary 2* 15:23-32.

———. 1989. *Feminist Utopias*. Lincoln: Univ. of Nebraska.

Bataille, Georges. 1986. *Eroticism: Death & Sensuality*. Trans. Mary Dalwood. San Francisco: City Lights Books.

Beaujour, Michel. 1987. "Flight Out of Time: Poetic Language and the Revolution." *Yale French Studies* 39:29-49.

Benhabib, Seyla. 1986. *Critique, Norm, and Utopia: A Study of the Foundations of Critical Theory*. New York: Columbia Univ.

Benveniste, Emil. 1971. *Problems in General Linguistics*. Trans. Mary Elizabeth Meek. Coral Gables: Univ. of Miami.

Bisseret, Noelle. 1979. *Education, Class Language and Ideology*. Boston: Routledge & Kegan Paul.

Blanchot, Maurice. 1986. *The Writing of the Disaster*. Trans. Ann Smock. Lincoln: Univ. of Nebraska.

Blevins, James L. 1984. *Revelation as Drama*. Nashville: Broadman.

Bloch, Ernst. 1971. *On Karl Marx*. Trans. John Maxwell. New York: Herder and Herder.

———. 1988. *The Utopian Function of Art and Literature*. Trans. Jack Zipes and Frank Mecklenburg. Cambridge: MIT.

Bloom, Harold. 1988. *Poetics of Influence*. New Haven: Henry R. Schwab.

Bloomfield, Morton W. 1961. *Piers Plowman as a Fourteenth-century Apocalypse*. New Brunswick: Rutgers Univ.

Boesak, Alan A. 1987. *Comfort and Protest: Reflections on the Apocalypse of John of Patmos*. Philadelphia: Westminster.

Bottingheimer, Ruth. 1980. "The Transformed Queen: A Search for the Origins of Negative Female Archetypes in Grimms' Fairy Tales." In *Gestaltet und Gestaltend: Frauen in der Deutschen Literatur*. Ed. Marianne Burkhard. Pp. 1-12. Amsterdam: Rodopi.

———. 1986. "Silenced Women in the Grimms' Tales: The "Fit" Between Fairy Tales and Society in Their Historical Context." In *Fairy Tales and Society: Illusion, Allusion, and Paradigm*. Ed. Ruth Bottingheimer. Pp. 115-131. Philadelphia: Univ. of Pennsylvania.

———. 1987. *Grimms' Bad Girls & Bad Boys: The Moral & Social Vision of the Tales*. New Haven: Yale Univ.

Bourdieu, Pierre. 1977. "Symbolic Power." In *Identity and Structure: Issues in the Sociology of Education*. Ed. Denis Gleeson. Pp. 113-119. Nafferton: Nafferton Books.

Brooke-Rose, Christine. 1981. *A Rhetoric of the Unreal: Studies in Narrative & Structure, Especially of the Fantastic*. Cambridge: Cambridge Univ.

Brooks, Peter. 1984. *Reading for the Plot: Design and Intention in Narrative*. New York: Alfred A. Knopf.

Brown, Norman. 1991. *Apocalypse and/or Metamorphosis*. Berkeley: Univ. of California.

Brownstein, Marilyn L. 1985. "Postmodern Language and the Perpetuation of Desire." *Twentieth Century Literature* 31:73-88.

Bryson, Norman. 1984. *Tradition and Desire: From David to Delacroix*.

Cambridge: Cambridge Univ.

Burke, Kenneth. 1963. "The Thinking of the Body: Comments on the Imagery of Catharsis in Literature." *Psychoanalytic Review* 50:25-68.

——. 1966. *Language as Symbolic Action: Essays on Life, Literature, and Method.* Berkeley: Univ. of California.

Butler, Judith P. 1987. *Subjects of Desire: Hegelian Reflections in Twentieth-Century France.* New York: Columbia Univ.

Byerman, Keith. 1989. "Desire and Alice Walker: The Quest for a Womanist Narrative." *Callaloo* 12:321-331.

Caldwell, Christopher. 1973. *Illusion and Reality: A Study of the Sources of Poetry.* New York: International Pubs.

Carroll, Noël. 1990. *The Philosophy of Horror or Paradoxes of the Heart.* New York: Routledge.

Carson, Anne. 1986. *Eros The Bittersweet: An Essay.* Princeton: Princeton Univ.

Chase, Cynthia. 1989. "Desire and Identification in Lacan and Kristeva." In *Feminism and Psychoanalysis.* Ed. Richard Feldstein and Judith Roof. Pp. 65-83. Ithaca: Cornell Univ.

Christ, Carol. 1987. *Laughter of Aphrodite: Reflections on a Journey to the Goddess.* San Francisco: Harper & Row.

Coward, Rosalind and John Ellis. 1977. *Language and Materialism: Developments in Semiology and the Theory of the Subject.* Boston: Routledge & Kegan Paul.

Culler, Jonathan. 1973. "Literary Fantasy." *Cambridge Review* 95:30-33.

——. 1982. *On Deconstruction: Theory and Criticism after Structuralism.* Ithaca: Cornell Univ.

Daly, Mary. 1984. *Pure Lust: Elemental Feminist Philosophy.* Boston: Beacon.

——. 1990. *Gyn-Ecology: The Metaethics of Radical Feminism.* Boston: Beacon.

Darton, Robert. 1984. *The Great Cat Massacre and Other Episodes in French Cultural History.* New York: Basic Books.

Derrida, Jacques. 1976. *Of Grammatology.* Trans. Gayatri Spivak. Baltimore: John Hopkins Univ.

——. 1981. *Positions.* Chicago: Univ. of Chicago.

——. 1982. "Of an Apocalyptic Tone Recently Adopted in Philosophy." Trans. John P. Leavy, Jr. *Semeia* 23:63-97.

——. 1984. "No Apocalypse, Not Now (full speed ahead, seven missiles, seven missives)." Trans. Catherine Porter and Philip Lewis. *Diacritics* 14:20-31.

——. 1987. *The Post Card: From Socrates to Freud and Beyond.* Trans. Alan Bass. Chicago: Univ. of Chicago.

Dowling, William C. 1984. *Jameson, Althusser, Marx: An Introduction to the Political Unconscious.* Ithaca: Cornell Univ.

Eagleton, Terry. 1976. *Criticism and Ideology: A Study in Marxist Literary Theory*. London: New Left Books.

——. 1983. *Literary Theory: An Introduction*. Minneapolis: Univ. of Minnesota.

——. 1990. *The Ideology of the Aesthetic*. Cambridge: Basil Blackwell.

——. 1991. *Ideology: An Introduction*. London: Verso.

Easthope, Antony C. 1983. *Poetry as Discourse*. New York: Methuen.

Eisenstein, Hester and Alice Jardine, eds. 1980. *The Future of Difference*. Boston: G. K. Hall.

Elliott, Robert C. 1970. *The Shape of Utopia: Studies in a Literary Genre*. Chicago: Univ. of Chicago.

Ellul, Jacques. 1977. *Apocalypse: The Book of Revelation*. G. W. Schreiner, trans. New York: Seabury.

Elshtain, Jean Bethke. 1987. *Women and War*. New York: Basic.

Eugene, Toinette M. 1984-1985. "Moral Values and Black Womanists." *Journal of Religious Thought* 41:23-34.

Foucault, Michel. 1972. *The Archeology of Knowledge*. Trans. A. M. Sheridan Smith. London: Pantheon.

Frappier-Mazur, Lucienne. 1988. "Marginal Canons: Rewriting the Erotic." *Yale French Studies* 75:112-128.

Fraser, Nancy. 1989. *Unruly Practices: Power, Discourse, and Gender in Contemporary Social Theory*. Minneapolis: Univ. of Minnesota.

Frow, John. 1986. *Marxism and Literary History*. Cambridge: Harvard Univ.

Frye, Northrop. 1957. *Anatomy of Criticism: Four Essays*. Princeton: Princeton Univ.

Füssel, Kuno. 1986. *Im Zeichen des Monstrums: Zur Staatskritik der Johannes-Apokalypse*. Freiburg: Edition Exodus.

Gadamer, Hans-Georg. 1975. *Truth and Method*. New York: Crossroad.

Gager, John. 1975. *Kingdom and Community: The Social World of Early Christianity*. Englewood Cliffs: Prentice-Hall.

Galbreath, Robert. 1988. "Fantastic Literature as Gnosis." *Extrapolation* 29:330-337.

Gallop, Jane. 1985. *Reading Lacan*. Ithaca: Cornell Univ.

——. 1989. "The Monster in the Mirror: The Feminist Critic's Psychoanalysis." In *Feminism and Psychoanalysis*. Ed. Richard Feldstein and Judith Roof. Pp. 13-24. Ithaca: Cornell Univ.

García-Treto, Francisco O. 1992. "The Fall of the House: A Carnivalesque Reading of 2 Kings 9 and 10." In *Reading Between Texts: Intertextuality and the Hebrew Bible*. D. N. Fewell, ed. Louisville: Westminster/John Knox. Pp. 153-71.

Gilman, Charlotte Perkins. 1979. *Herland*. New York: Pantheon.

Girard, René. 1965. *Deceit, Desire, and the Novel: Self and Other in Literary Structure*. Trans. Yvonne Freccero. Baltimore: Johns Hopkins.

———. 1977. *Violence and the Sacred*. Trans. Patrick Gregory. Baltimore: Johns Hopkins Univ.

———. 1986. *The Scapegoat*. Trans. Yvonne Freccero. Baltimore: Johns Hopkins Univ.

Girgus, Sam B. 1990. *Desire and the Political Unconscious in American Literature: Eros and Ideology*. New York: St. Martin's.

Goldman, Lucien. 1964. *The Hidden God*. Boston: Routledge & Kegan Paul.

Goldstein, Philip. 1990. *The Politics of Literary Theory: An Introduction to Marxist Criticism*. Tallahassee: Florida State Univ.

Goodheart, Eugene. 1991. *Desire and Its Discontents*. New York: Columbia Univ.

Gramsci, Antonio. 1978. *Selections from the Prison Notebooks*. Ed. and trans. Quintin Hoare and Geoffrey Nowell Smith. New York: International Pubs.

Greene, Gayle and Coppelia Kahn. 1985. "Feminist Scholarship and the Social Construction of Woman." In *Making a Difference: Feminist Literary Criticism*. Eds. Greene and Kahn. Pp. 1-36. New York: Routledge.

Griffin, Susan. 1981. *Pornography and Silence: Culture's Revenge against Nature*. New York: Harper & Row.

Grixti, Joseph. 1989. *Terrors of Uncertainty: The Cultural Contexts of Horror Fiction*. London: Routledge.

Grosz, Elizabeth. 1989. *Sexual Subversions: Three French Feminists*. Sydney: Allen & Unwin.

———. 1990. *Jacques Lacan: A Feminist Introduction*. New York: Routledge.

Guattari, Felix. 1979. "A Liberation of Desire." Interview with George Stambolian. Trans. G. Stambolian. In *Homosexualities and French Literature: Cultural Contexts/Critical Texts*. Ed. George Stambolian and Elaine Marks. Pp. 56-69. Ithaca: Cornell Univ.

Halliday, M. A. K. 1978. *Language as Social Semiotic*. London: Edward Arnold.

Hallissy, Margaret. 1987. *Venomous Woman: Fear of the Female in Literature*. New York: Greenwood.

Halperin, David M., John J. Winkler, and Froma I. Zeitlin, eds. 1990. *Before Sexuality: The Construction of Erotic Experience in the Ancient Greek World*. Princeton: Princeton Univ.

Harlow, Barbara. 1987. *Resistance Literature*. New York: Methuen.

Harris, Michael. 1988a. "Deceit, Desire, and Violence: A Critique of Girard's Reading of the Apocalypse." Unpublished manuscript.

———. 1988b. "The Literary Function of Hymns in the Apocalypse of John." Ph.D. Southern Baptist Theological Seminary.

———. 1989. "Text in Vision/Vision in Text: Toward an 'Open' Poetics for the Apocalypse of John." Unpublished manuscript.

Hassan, Ihab. 1984. "Parabiography: The Varieties of Critical Experience." In *American Critics at Work: Examinations of Contemporary Literary Theories*. Ed. Victor A. Kramer. Pp. 421-442. New York: Whitston.

Hemer, Colin J. 1989. *The Letters to the Seven Churches of Asia in their Local Setting*. Sheffield: Univ. of Sheffield.

Hirst, Paul. 1979. *On Law and Ideology*. New York: Macmillan.

Hoch-Smith, Judith and Anita Spring. 1978. "Introduction." In *Women in Ritual and Symbolic Roles*. Eds. Hoch-Smith and Spring. Pp. 1-23. New York: Plenum.

Hopkins, Keith. 1983. *Death and Renewal*. New York: Cambridge Univ.

Horn, Pierre L. and Mary Beth Pringle. 1984. "Introduction." In *The Image of the Prostitute in Modern Literature*. Eds. Horn and Pringle. Pp. 1-7. New York: Frederick Ungar.

Hume, Catherine. 1984. *Fantasy and Mimesis: Responses to Reality in Western Literature*. New York: Methuen.

Hunter, Diane, ed. 1989. *Seduction and Theory: Readings of Gender, Representation, and Rhetoric*. Urbana: Univ. of Illinois.

Huntington, Richard and Peter Metcalf. 1979. *Celebrations of Death: The Anthropology of Mortuary Rituals*. Cambridge: Cambridge Univ.

Huston, Nancy. 1982. "Tales of War and Tears of Women." *Women's Studies International Forum* 5:271-282.

Irwin, W. R. 1976. *The Game of the Impossible: A Rhetoric of Fantasy*. Chicago: Univ. of Illinois.

Jackson, Rosemary. 1981. *Fantasy: The Literature of Subversion*. New York: Methuen.

Jacobus, Mary. 1982. "Is There a Woman in this Text?" *New Literary History* 14:117-141.

Jameson, Fredric. 1971. *Marxism and Form*. Princeton: Princeton Univ.

——. 1972. *The Prison-House of Language: A Critical Account of Structural and Russian Formalism*. Princeton: Princeton Univ.

——. 1981. *The Political Unconscious: Narrative as a Socially Symbolic Act*. Ithaca: Cornell Univ.

——. 1991. *Postmodernism, or The Cultural Logic of Late Capitalism*. Durham: Duke Univ.

Jardine, Alice. 1986. "Death Sentences: Writing Couples and Ideology." In *The Female Body in Western Culture*. Ed. Susan Rubin Suleiman. Pp. 84-96. Cambridge: Harvard Univ.

Jay, Martin. 1984. *Marxism & Totality: The Adventures of a Concept from Lukacs to Habermas*. Berkeley: Univ. of California.

Jay, Nancy. 1985. "Sacrifice as Remedy for Having Been Born of Woman." In *Immaculate and Powerful: The Female in Sacred Image and Social Reality*. Eds. Clarissa W. Atkinson, et. al. Pp. 283-309. Boston: Beacon.

Johnson, Barbara. 1980. *The Critical Difference: Essays in the Contemporary Rhetoric of Reading.* Baltimore: Johns Hopkins Univ.

Jones, Libby Falk and Sarah Webster Goodwin, eds. 1990. *Feminism, Utopia, and Narrative.* Knoxville: Univ. of Tennessee.

Kamuf, Peggy. 1982. *Fictions of Feminine Desire: Disclosures of Heloise.* Lincoln: Univ. of Nebraska.

Kauffman, Linda S. 1986. *Discourses of Desire: Gender, Genre, and Epistolary Fiction.* Ithaca: Cornell Univ.

Kearney, Richard. *The Wake of the Imagination: Toward a Postmodern Culture.* Minneapolis: Univ. of Minnesota.

Keller, Catherine. 1990. "Warriors, Women, and the Nuclear Complex: Toward a Postnuclear Postmodernity." In *Sacred Connections: Postmodern Spirituality, Political Economy, and Art.* Ed. David Ray Griffin. Pp. 63-82. Albany: State Univ. of New York.

Keohane, Nannerl O., Michelle Z. Rosaldo, and Barbara C. Gelpi, eds. 1981. *Feminist Theory: A Critique of Ideology.* Chicago: The Univ. of Chicago.

Ketterer, David. 1974. *New Worlds for Old: The Apocalyptic Imagination, Science Fiction and American Literature.* Bloomington: Indiana Univ.

Koelb, Clayton. 1984. *The Incredulous Reader: Literature and the Function of Disbelief.* Ithaca: Cornell Univ.

Kolodny, Annette. 1975. *The Lay of the Land: Metaphor as Experience and History in American Life and Letters.* Chapel Hill: Univ. of North Carolina.

Kraemer, Heinrich. 1951. *Malleus Maleficarum.* London: Pushkin.

Kreuziger, Frederick A. 1982. *Apocalypse and Science Fiction: A Dialectic of Religious and Secular Soteriologies.* Chico: Scholars.

Kristeva, Julia. 1980. *Desire in Language.* New York: Columbia Univ.

———. 1982. *Powers of Horror: An Essay on Abjection.* New York: Columbia Univ.

Lacan, Jacques. 1977. "Desire and the Interpretation of Desire in *Hamlet.*" *Yale French Studies* 55-56:11-52.

Landy, Marcia. 1977. "The Silent Woman: Towards a Feminist Critique." In *The Authority of Experience: Essays in Feminist Criticism.* Eds. Arlyn Diamond and Lee R. Edwards. Pp. 16-27. Amherst: Univ. of Massachusetts.

Lefanu, Sarah. 1988. *Feminism and Science Fiction.* Bloomington: Indiana Univ.

Lesser, Simon. 1957. *Fiction and the Unconscious.* Boston: Beacon.

Linton, Gregory. 1991. "Reading the Apocalypse as an Apocalypse." In *Society of Biblical Literature 1991 Seminar Papers.* Ed. Eugene H. Lovering. Pp. 161-186. Atlanta: Scholars.

Loraux, Nicole. 1987. *Tragic Ways of Killing a Woman.* Cambridge: Harvard Univ.

Lovecraft, H. P. 1973. *Supernatural Horror in Literature.* Ed. E. F.

Bleiler. New York: Dover.

Lukács, Georg. 1962. *The Historical Novel.* London: Merlin.

Lüthi, Max. 1984. *The Fairytale as Art Form and Portrait of Man.* Trans. Jon Erickson. Bloomington: Indiana Univ.

Macdonell, Diane. 1986. *Theories of Discourse: An Introduction.* New York: Basil Blackwell.

McGinn, Bernard. 1983. "Symbols of the Apocalypse in Medieval Culture." *Michigan Quarterly Review* 22:265-283.

Macherey, Pierre. 1978. *A Theory of Literary Production.* Trans. Geoffrey Wall. New York: Routledge & Kegan Paul.

Maclean, Marie. 1987. "Oppositional Practices in Women's Traditional Practices." *New Literary History* 19:37-50.

Macy, Joanna. 1987. "Learning to Sustain the Gaze." In *Facing Apocalypse.* Eds. Valerie Andrews, Robert Bosnak, and Karen Walter Goodwin. Pp. 164-169. Dallas: Spring.

Manlove, C. N. 1982. "On the Nature of Fantasy." In *The Aesthetics of Fantasy in Literature and Art.* Ed. Roger C. Schlobin. Pp. 16-35. Notre Dame: Univ. of Notre Dame.

———. 1983. *The Impulse of Fantasy Literature.* Kent: Kent State Univ.

Mannheim, Karl. 1936. *Ideology and Utopia.* Trans. Louis Wirth and Edward Shils. New York: Harcourt, Brace & World.

Marx, Karl. 1977. *Karl Marx: Selected Writings.* Ed. David McClellan. New York: Oxford Univ.

Meese, Elizabeth. 1992. "The Erotics of the Letter." *South Atlantic Review* 57:11-28.

———. 1992. *(Sem)erotics: Theorizing Lesbian Writing.* New York: New York Univ.

Miller, J. Hillis. 1987. "Presidential Address 1986: The Triumph of Theory, the Resistance to Reading, and the Question of the Material Base." *PMLA* 102:281-291.

Mohanty, Chandra Talpade, Ann Russo, and Lourdes Torres, eds. 1991. *Third World Women and the Politics of Feminism.* Bloomington: Indiana Univ.

Moi, Toril. 1982. "The Missing Mother: The Oedipal Rivalries of Rene Girard." *Diacritics* 12:21-31.

———. 1985. *Sexual/Textual Politics: Feminist Literary Theory.* New York: Methuen.

Moore, Stephen D. 1989. *Literary Criticism and the Gospels: The Theoretical Challenge.* New Haven: Yale Univ.

———. 1992. *Mark and Luke in Poststructuralist Perspectives: Jesus Begins to Write.* New Haven: Yale Univ.

Mortimer, Armine Kotin. 1991. *Plotting to Kill.* New York: Peter Lang.

Moylan, Tom. 1986. *Demand the Impossible: Science Fiction and the Utopian Imagination.* New York: Methuen.

Newton, Judith and Deborah Rosenfelt. 1985. *Feminist Criticism and Social Change: Sex, Class and Race in Literature and Culture.*

New York: Methuen.

Niebuhr, Reinhold. 1932. *Moral Man and Immoral Society*. New York: Charles Scribner's Sons.

O'Connor, Flannery. 1957. *Mystery and Manners*. Eds. Sally and Robert Fitzgerald. New York: Straus & Giroux.

Olsen, Lance. 1987. *Ellipse of Uncertainty: An Introduction to Postmodern Fantasy*. New York: Greenwood.

Orwell, George. 1949. *Nineteen Eighty-Four*. New York: Harcourt, Brace & World.

Oxenhandler, Neal. 1988. "The Changing Concept of Literary Emotion: A Selective History." *New Literary History* 20:102-121.

Palumbo, Donald. 1986. "Sexuality and the Allure of the Fantastic in Literature." In *Erotic Universe: Sexuality and Fantastic in Literature*. Ed. Donald Palumbo. Pp. 3-24. New York: Greenwood.

Prendergast, Christopher. 1986. *The Order of Mimesis: Balzac, Stendhal, Nerval, Flaubert*. Cambridge: Cambridge Univ.

Propp, Vladimir. 1978. *"Structure and History in the Study of the Fairy Tale."* Semeia 10:57-83.

Pozzi, Dora C. and John M. Wickersham, eds. 1991. *Myth and the Polis*. Ithaca: Cornell Univ.

Rabinowitz, Peter J. 1987. *Before Reading: Narrative Conventions and the Politics of Interpretation*. Ithaca: Cornell Univ.

Rabkin, Eric S. 1976. *The Fantastic in Literature*. Princeton: Princeton Univ.

Ragland-Sullivan, Ellie. 1989. "Seeking the Third Term: Desire, the Phallus, and the Materiality of Language." In *Feminism and Psychoanalysis*. Ed. Richard Feldstein and Judith Roof. Pp. 40-64. Ithaca: Cornell Univ.

Ramazanoglu, Caroline. 1989. *Feminism and the Contradictions of Oppression*. New York: Routledge.

Rich, Adrienne. 1984. *The Fact of a Doorframe: Poems Selected and New 1950-1984*. New York: W. W. Norton.

Ricoeur, Paul. 1988. *Lectures on Ideology and Utopia*. Ed. George Taylor. New York: Columbia Univ.

Rosenau, Pauline Marie. 1992. *Post-Modernism and the Social Sciences: Insights, Inroads, and Intrusions*. Princeton: Princeton Univ.

Rosinsky, Natalie M. 1984. *Feminist Futures: Contemporary Women's Speculative Fiction*. Ann Arbor: UMI Research.

Rowe, Karen E. 1979. "Feminism and Fairy Tales." *Women's Studies* 6:237-257.

———. 1986. "To Spin a Yarn: The Female Voice in Folklore and Fairy Tale." In *Fairy Tales and Society: Illusion, Allusion, and Paradigm*. Ed. Ruth Bottigheimer. Pp. 53-74. Philadelphia: Univ. of Pennsylvania.

Rowland, Christopher and Mark Corner. 1989. *Liberating Exegesis: The Challenge of Liberation Theology to Biblical Studies*. Louisville: Westminster/John Knox.

Russ, Joanna. 1972. "The Image of Women in Science Fiction." In *Images of Women in Fiction: Feminist Perspectives*. Ed. Susan Koppelman Cornillon. Pp. 79-94. Bowling Green: Bowling Green Univ.

Ryan, Michael. 1982. *Marxism and Deconstruction: A Critical Articulation*. Baltimore: Johns Hopkins.

Sankovitch, Tilde A. *French Women Writers and the Book: Myths of Access and Desire*. Syracuse: Syracuse Univ.

Scarry, Elaine. 1985. *The Body in Pain: The Making and Unmaking of the World*. New York: Oxford Univ.

Schell, Jonathan. 1982. *The Fate of the Earth*. New York: Avon.

Scheff, T. J. 1979. *Catharsis in Healing, Ritual, and Drama*. Berkeley: Univ. of California.

Schleifer, Ronald. 1990. *Rhetoric and Death: The Language of Modernism and Postmodern Discourse Theory*. Urbana: Univ. of Illinois.

Schlobin, Roger C. 1988. "Children of a Darker God: A Taxonomy of Deep Horror Fiction and Film and their Mass Popularity." *Journal of the Fantastic in the Arts* 1:25-50.

Scholes, Robert. 1975. *Structural Fabulation: An Essay on Fiction of the Future*. Notre Dame: Univ. of Notre Dame.

———. 1981. "A Footnote to Russ's "Recent Feminist Utopias."" In *Future Females: A Critical Anthology*. Ed. Marleen S. Barr. Pp. 86-87. Bowling Green: Bowling Green Univ.

Schüssler Fiorenza, Elisabeth. 1981. *Invitation to the Book of Revelation*. New York: Doubleday.

———. 1985. *The Book of Revelation: Justice and Judgement*. Philadelphia: Fortress.

———. 1991. *Revelation: Vision of a Just World*. Minneapolis: Fortress.

Schweickart, Patrocinio P. 1986. "Reading Ourselves: Toward a Feminist Theory of Reading." In *Gender and Reading: Essays on Readers, Text, and Contexts*. Eds. Elizabeth A. Flynn and Patrocinio P. Schweickart. Pp. 31-62. Baltimore: Johns Hopkins.

Seeley, David. 1990. *The Noble Death: Graeco-Roman Martyrology and Paul's Concept of Salvation*. Sheffield: Sheffield Univ.

Selden, Raman. 1985 and 1989. *A Reader's Guide to Contemporary Literary Theory*. Lexington: Univ. of Kentucky.

Siebers, Tobin. 1984. *The Romantic Fantastic*. Ithaca: Cornell Univ.

———. 1988. *The Ethics of Criticism*. Ithaca: Cornell Univ.

Spacks, Patricia Meyer. 1990. *Desire and Truth: Functions of Plot in Eighteenth-Century English Novels*. Chicago: Univ. of Chicago.

Spence, Sarah. 1988. *Rhetorics of Reason and Desire: Vergil, Augustine, and the Troubadours*. Ithaca: Cornell Univ.

Spivak, Gayatri C. 1983. "Displacement and the Discourse of Woman." In *Displacement: Derrida and After*. Ed. Mark Krupnick. Pp.

169-195. Bloomington: Indiana Univ.

———. 1987. *In Other Worlds: Essays in Cultural Politics*. New York: Methuen.

———. 1988. "Can the Subaltern Speak?" In *Marxism and the Interpretation of Culture*. Eds. Cary Nelson and Lawrence Grossberg. Pp. 271-313. Urbana: Univ. of Illinois.

Stanton, Elizabeth Cady. 1974. *The Woman's Bible*. Seattle: Coalition Task Force on Women and Religion.

Stone, Kay. 1985. "The Misuses of Enchantment." In *Women's Folklore, Women's Culture*. Eds. Rosan Jordan and Susan Kalcik. Pp. 125-145. Philadelphia: Univ. of Pennsylvania.

———. 1986. "Feminist Approaches to the Interpretation of Fairy Tales." In *Fairy Tales and Society: Illusion, Allusion, and Paradigm*. Ed. Ruth Bottingheimer. Pp. 229-235. Philadelphia: Univ. of Pennsylvania.

Tatar, Maria. 1987. *The Hard Facts of the Grimms' Fairy Tales*. Princeton: Princeton Univ.

Tavis, Anna. 1986. "Fairy Tales from a Semiotic Perspective." In *Fairy Tales and Society: Illusion, Allusion, and Paradigm*. Ed. Ruth Bottingheimer. Pp. 195-202. Philadelphia: Univ. of Pennsylvania.

Thompson, J. B. 1984. *Studies in the Theory of Ideology*. Berkeley: Univ. of California.

———. 1990. *Ideology and Modern Culture*. Stanford: Stanford Univ.

Thompson, Leonard. 1990. *The Book of Revelation: Apocalypse and Empire*. New York: Oxford Univ.

Todorov, Tzvetan. 1973. *The Fantastic: A Structural Approach to a Literary Genre*. Trans. Richard Howard. Ithaca: Cornell Univ.

Toynbee, J. M. C. 1971. *Death and Burial in the Roman World*. Ithaca: Cornell Univ.

Trinh T. Minh-Ha. 1990. "Not You/Like You: Post-Colonial Women and the Interlocking Questions of Identity and Difference." In *Making Face, Making Soul=Haciendo caras*. Ed. Gloria Anzaldúa. Pp. 371-375. San Francisco: Aunt Lute Foundation.

Turner, Victor. 1969. *The Ritual Process*. Chicago: Aldine.

van der Meer, Frederick. 1978. *Apocalypse: Visions from the Book of Revelation in Western Art*. London: Thames and Hudson.

Vergote, Antoine. 1988. *Guilt and Desire: Religious Attitudes and Their Pathological Derivatives*. Trans. M. H. Wood. New Haven: Yale Univ.

Vitz, Evelyn Birge. 1989. *Medieval Narrative and Modern Narratology: Subjects and Objects of Desire*. New York: New York Univ.

von Franz, Marie-Louise. 1972. *The Feminine in Fairytales*. Dallas: Spring.

Walhout, Clarence. 1986. "Marxist and Christian Hermeneutics: A Study of Jameson's *The Political Unconscious*." *Faith and Philosophy* 3:135-155.

Walker, Alice. 1982. "Only Justice Can Stop a Curse." In *Reweaving the Web of Life: Feminism and Nonviolence.* Ed. Pam McAllister. Pp. 262-265. Philadelphia: New Society.

Weber, Eugene. 1981. "Fairies and Hard Facts: The Reality of Folktales." *Journal of the History of Ideas* 42:93-113.

Weedon, Chris. 1987. *Feminist Practice and Poststructuralist Theory.* New York: Basil Blackwell.

Welch, Sharon D. 1985. *Communities of Resistance and Solidarity: A Feminist Theology of Liberation.* Maryknoll: Orbis.

West, Cornel. 1983. "Fredric Jameson's Marxist Hermeneutics." *Boundary* 2:177-200.

Winnett, Susan. 1990. "Coming Unstrung: Women, Men, Narrative, and Principles of Pleasure." *PMLA* 105/3:505-518.

Wolfe, Gary. 1982. "The Encounter with Fantasy." In *The Aesthetics of Fantasy Literature and Art.* Ed. Roger C. Schlobin. Pp. 1-15. Notre Dame: Univ. of Notre Dame.

Wyatt, Jean. 1990. *Reconstructing Desire: The Role of the Unconscious in Women's Reading and Writing.* Chapel Hill: Univ. of North Carolina.

Yarbro Collins, Adela. 1976. *The Combat Myth in the Book of Revelation.* Missoula: Scholars.

——. 1979. *The Apocalypse.* Wilmington: Michael Glazier.

——. 1980. "Revelation 18: Taunt-Song or Dirge?" In *L'Apocalypse johannique et l'apocalypstique dans le Nouveau Testament.* Ed. Jan Lambrecht. Pp. 185-204. Louvain: Louvain Univ.

——. 1981. "The Revelation of John: An Apocalyptic Response to a Social Crisis." *Currents in Theology and Mission* 8:4-12.

——. 1983. "Persecution and Vengeance in the Book of Revelation." In *Apocalypticism in the Mediterranean World and the Near East.* Ed. David Hellholm. Pp. 729-749. Tubingen: Mohr-Siebeck.

——. 1984. *Crisis and Catharsis: The Power of the Apocalypse.* Philadelphia: Westminster.

——. 1985. "Insiders and Outsiders in the Book of Revelation and Its Social Context." In *"To See Ourselves As Others See Us." Christians, Jews, "Others" in Late Antiquity.* Ed. Jacob Neusner and Ernest S. Frerichs. Pp. 187-218. Chico: Scholars.

——. 1987. "Women's History and the Book of Revelation." *Society of Biblical Literature 1987 Seminar Papers.* Ed. Kent Howard Richards. Pp. 80-91. Atlanta: Scholars.

Zanger, Jules. 1982. "Heroic Fantasy and Social Reality: ex nihilo nihil fit." In *The Aesthetics of Fantasy in Literature and Art.* Ed. Roger C. Schlobin. Pp. 226-236. Notre Dame: Univ. of Notre Dame.

Zipes, Jack. 1986a. "Marxists and the Illumination of Folk and Fairy Tales." In *Fairy Tales and Society: Illusion, Allusion, and Paradigm.* Ed. R. Bottigheimer. Pp. 235-243. Philadelphia: Univ. of Pennsylvania.

——. 1986b. *Fairy Tales and the Art of Subversion: The Classical Genre for Children and the Process of Civilization.* New York: Wildman.

INDEXES

AUTHORS

Abdulla, Adnan 17, 111
Abrams, M. H. 113-114
Allen, V. 73
Althusser, Louis 72
Anzaldúa, Gloria 48-49, 77, 79-80
Bakhtin, Mikhail 27, 65-67, 95
Barthes, Roland 27, 30, 105
Bataille, Georges 22
Beaujour, Michel 93-94
Benveniste, Emile 112
Berrigan, Daniel 51
Blanchot, Maurice 39, 49
Bloch, Ernst 39-40, 95, 113
Boesak, Alan 51, 54-55
Bottigheimer, Ruth 65, 77, 115
Brooke-Rose, Christine 95, 116
Brooks, Peter 83
Brown, Norman O. 45
Burke, Kenneth 17
Butler, Judith 85-86
Cardenal, Ernesto 51
Carroll, Noël 90
Cassirer, Ernst 111
Christ, Carol 79
Cixous, Hélène 92, 97, 116
Coward, Rosalind 29
Culler, Jonathan 104
Daly, Mary 81

Deleuze, Gilles 113
Derrida, Jacques 22, 38, 82, 88, 111
Dowling, William C. 113
Eagleton, Terry 29, 30, 64, 111, 112, 113
Ellis, John 29
Ellul, Jacques 111
Elshtain, Jean 100
Eugene, Toinette M. 101
Foucault, Michel 111, 113
Frost, Robert 10
Frow, John 20, 38
Frye, Northrop 27, 41, 93
Gadamer, Hans-Georg 33, 113
Gage, Matilda Joslyn 48
Gager, John 19-20
Gallop, Jane 85
Gilman, Charlotte Perkins 105, 106
Girard, René 18, 43, 84
Girgus, Sam 22, 114
Golden, Leon 111
Goodheart, Eugene 85
Gramsci, Antonio 54
Greimas, A. J. 31-32, 34
Griffin, Susan 98
Grosz, Elizabeth 35, 85
Guattari, Felix 113
Halliday, M. A. K. 20
Harlow, Barbara 112
Harris, Michael 84, 88

Hoch-Smith, Judith 103-104, 115
Hopkins, Keith 61-62
Horn, Pierre L. 59, 61
Hume, Katherine 41, 116
Hunter, Diane 86
Jackson, Rosemary 42-43, 65, 89, 94, 95, 100
Jameson, Fredric 21, 23, 27, 29, 31-41, 104, 111, 112, 113
Jardine, Alice 97-98
Jay, Martin 112
Johnson, Barbara 24
Kearney, Richard 82
Keller, Catherine 48, 78, 101
Koelb, Clayton 95
Kolodny, Annette 88
Kraemer, Heinrich 81
Lacan, Jacques 21, 85, 87, 97
Landy, Marcia 115
Lefanu, Sarah 76
LeGuin, Ursula 105
Loraux, Nicole 60-61
Lovecraft, H. P. 90
Macherey, Pierre 30
Macy, Joanna 101
Manlove, Colin 42
Marx, Karl 28, 35
Mohanty, Chandra Talpade 114
Moi, Toril 23, 84, 92-93, 116
Moore, Stephen 112
Newton, Judith 59, 60, 86, 98
Niebuhr, Reinhold 36-37
Nietzsche, Frederich 31
Olson, Lance 71
Orwell, George 54
Oxenhandler, Neal 85
Palumbo, Donald 74

Paul, T. 73
Piercy, Marge 70, 105
Pringle, Mary Beth 59, 61
Rabinowitz, Peter 27, 87
Ricoeur, Paul 64
Rosenau, Pauline Marie 111
Rosenfelt, Deborah 59, 60, 86, 98
Rowe, Karen 75
Ruether, Rosemary Radford 45
Russ, Joanna 69-70
Sankovitch, Tilde 83-84
Scheff, T. J. 17
Schell, Jonathan 101
Scholes, Robert 69, 83, 96
Schüssler Fiorenza, Elisabeth 46, 49, 51-53, 83, 115-116, 116
Schweickart, Patrocinio 26
Seeley, David 62-63
Selden, Raman 34
Siebers, Tobin 42-43, 94
Spence, Sarah 85
Spivak, Gayatri Chakravorty 54, 106, 112, 115
Spring, Anita 103-104, 115
Todorov, Tzvetan 41-42, 71, 89, 114
Trinh T. Minh-ha 114
Turner, Victor 64
van der Meer, Frederick 111
Walker, Alice 100-101
Weber, Eugene 77
Welch, Sharon 116
West, Cornel 35, 113
Wiesel, Elie 112-113
Winnett, Susan 83
Wolfe, Gary K. 114
Yarbro Collins, Adela 19, 49-50, 53, 55, 56, 70, 75-76
Zipes, Jack 40-41

APOCALYPSE OF JOHN

Apocalypse 1
1:1 96
1:9 56, 99
1:12-16 31, 90
1:17 90

Apocalypse 2
2:1 31
2:7 18, 97
2:8 31
2:11 97
2:12 31
2:17 18, 97
2:18 31
2:20 28
2:22-23 72
2:26 97
2:26-28 18-19

Apocalypse 3
—— 18
3:1 31
3:5 97
3:7 31
3:12 19, 97
3:14 31
3:15 19
3:21 19, 97

Apocalypse 4
4:1-5:14 19

Apocalypse 5
5:2 58
5:6 18
5:12 58, 91

Apocalypse 6
6:1-17 20

6:9 18
6:16-17 99

Apocalypse 7
7:1-8:4 19
7:2 91
7:4-8 55
7:9 55
7:14 18, 93

Apocalypse 8
8:5-9:21 20

Apocalypse 9
9:21 28

Apocalypse 10
10:1-11:1 19
10:2 91
10:11 63

Apocalypse 11
—— 58, 60, 62
11:2-14 20
11:3 63
11:6 63
11:8 63
11:9 63
11:10 63
11:13 64
11:15-19 19

Apocalypse 12
—— 20, 34, 53,
      65, 75-76,
      79, 84
12:1-17 20
12:1 74
12:5 75

12:6 76
12:10 91
12:12 20
12:13 75, 77
12:14 72, 76
12:16 79

Apocalypse 13
—— 20
13:1-2 20
13:1-18 90
13:11 90

Apocalypse 14
—— 35
14:1-5 50
14:1-7 19
14:4 50, 70
14:5 71
14:8 28
14:8-15:1 20
14:9-11 20-21
14:15 91
14:18 91

Apocalypse 15
15:2-8 19
15:16 91

Apocalypse 16
16:1-20 20
16:1 91
16:19 65

Apocalypse 17
—— 58, 60
17:1-18:24 20
17:1 65
17:3 81

Apocalypse 17
[cont.]
17:3b-6 57
17:5 65
17:6 65, 66-67,
    68, 86, 90
17:7 57
17:16 57, 67-
    68, 81, 98

Apocalypse 18
—— 58, 60, 93
18:2 72
18:3a 86
18:4 28, 82
18:7 65
18:8 67
18:9 67
18:10 61, 67
18:11-17 68
18:14-15 61
18:16-17 61
18:17 29, 67
18:19 29, 67
18:19-20 61
18:21 67

18:21-24 62
18:24 68, 86

Apocalypse 19
19:1-8 62
19:1-16 19
19:3 67
19:7 68
19:7-8 62
19:8 68
19:9 68, 86,
    106
19:11 99
19:13 99
19:14 100
19:15a-b 100
19:16 99
19:17-18 68
19:17-21 61
19:17-20:15 20
19:21 68, 100

Apocalypse 20
—— 45, 93
20:10 99
20:14 62, 93
20:15 35, 99

Apocalypse 21
21:1-22:5 19
21:1 99
21:2 72, 80
21:3-5a 92
21:4 62, 102
21:5 89, 95
21:7 29, 93
21:8 55, 56, 62,
    93
21:9-10 99
21:11 93
21:26 93
21:27 93

Apocalypse 22
22:3 55, 93
22:6 95, 96
22:10-11 87
22:10 94
22:14 29, 93
22:15 29, 55,
    93
22:17 82, 94
22:18-19 89
22:20 39

From the *Hortus deliciarum* (late 12th century). The winged woman with the crescent moon at her feet gives up her child to the angel. She represents the Church. The dragon, left, is murdering the saints; right, the dragon spits water, his tail sending the stars, the fallen angels, to earth.

"But her child was snatched away and taken to God and to his throne; and the woman fled to the wilderness, where she has a place prepared by God . . . Then the dragon was angry with the woman, and went off to make war on the rest of her children, those who keep the commandments of God and hold the testimony of Jesus." (Apocalypse 12:5-6, 17)

William Blake, *The Great Red Dragon and the Woman Clothed with the Sun* (Rosenwald Collection, © 1992 National Gallery of Art, Washington, c. 1805, Pen and ink with watercolor over graphite, Bible for Thomas Butts, Butlin 1989). This captures the moment of terror, when the winged woman is confronted by the dragon. The woman is light; the dragon is darker. Her outstretched wings and arms depict power.

"It should not be possible in the late twentieth century to continue to ignore the institutions of terror that have circumscribed the experience of women over the centuries . . ." — John Winkler.

Odilon Redon, *The Apocalyptic Woman* (1899), also shows the woman in a sphere of light. The darkness surrounding her is almost overwhelming—"almost" because she resolutely faces the unknown. Are her arms raised in fear or flight?

"If you can't be free, be a mystery" — Rita Dove.

[Opposite]
Albrecht Dürer's depiction of the Whore of Babylon belongs in a sequence of 15 woodcuts on the Apocalypse (1496-98). The Whore, beautifully adorned, but obviously drunk, rides the beast for the last time as Babylon is destroyed behind her. She holds the cup of abominations and is worshiped and admired by the crowd, including rulers and clerics, who represent the immorality of church and government. (In Cranach's 1535 woodcut for the Luther Bible she wears the papal tiara, removed in later editions.) The angel prepares to throw the millstone.

"And I saw a woman sitting on a scarlet beast that was full of blasphemous names, and it had seven heads and ten horns. The woman was clothed in purple and scarlet, and adorned with gold and jewels and pearls, holding in her hand a golden cup full of abominations and the impurities of her fornication; and on her forehead was written a name, a mystery: 'Babylon the great, mother of whores and of earth's abomination.' And I saw the woman was drunk with the blood of the witnesses to Jesus. When I saw her, I was greatly amazed. But the angel said to me, 'Why are you so amazed?'" (Apocalypse 17:3-7a)

"The future can only be anticipated in the form of an absolute danger. It is that which breaks absolutely with the constituted normality and can only be proclaimed, *presented*, as a sort of monstrosity." — Jacques Derrida

❦

[Following page]
In this 17th century copy of the *Hortus deliciarum* the great Whore and the beast are thrown into the lake of fire by two angels with pitchforks. The kings, merchants, the pope, and the religious lament her death. In her drunken state, the Whore smiles as she is stabbed and burned, dropping the cup full of abominations.

"The merchants of these wares, who gained wealth from her, will stand far off, in fear of her torment, weeping and mourning aloud . . . for in one hour all this wealth has been laid waste." (Apocalypse 18:15-16)

"Then a mighty angel took up a stone like a great millstone and threw it into the sea, saying, 'With such violence Babylon the great city will be thrown down, and will be found no more.'" (Apocalypse 18:21)

[Overleaf, top]
Agenore Fabbri's *The Whore of Babylon* (1950) shows men gazing on the naked body of the Whore as she reclines on a bed.

"But I have this against you: you tolerate that woman Jezebel, who calls herself a prophet and is teaching and beguiling my servants to practice fornication and to eat food sacrificed to idols. I gave her time to repent, but she refuses to repent of her fornication. Beware, I am throwing her on a bed, and those who commit adultery with her I am throwing into great distress, unless they repent of her doings; and I will strike her children dead." (Apocalypse 2:20-23a)

"Come out of her, my people, so that you do not take part in her sins, and so that you do not share in her plagues; for her sins are heaped high as heaven and God has remembered her iniquities." (Apocalypse 18:4-5)

❦

[Overleaf, bottom]
This lithograph by Lovis Corinth (1916), from a sequence of six, graphically depicts the destruction of the Whore of Babylon. In the previous picture the Whore is made "desolate and naked." Here the kings eat her, pulling great hunks of flesh from her body. She is smiling.

"And the ten horns that you saw, where the whore is seated, are peoples and multitudes and nations and languages. And the ten horns that you saw, they and the beast will hate the whore; they will make her desolate and naked; they will devour her flesh and burn her up with fire." (Apocalypse 17:16)

"A laughing apocalypse is an apocalypse without God."
— Julia Kristeva

In *Christ Sees the New Jerusalem* (1860) Julius Schnorr von Carolsfeld presents an image of the Bride as beautiful and reserved. She is prepared for the marriage by the angels. And all of heaven rejoices.

"And I saw the holy city, the new Jerusalem, coming down out of heaven from God, prepared as a bride adorned for her husband."

(Apocalypse 21:2)

In Max Beckmann's *The Sounding of the Fifth and Sixth Trumpet* (1943), beasts destroy people. The cartoonish dimensions exaggerate the juxtaposition of sexuality and death. At the bottom a naked female body, wearing only a necklace and shoes, is attacked. There is a death struggle; humanity is destroyed.

"And in those days people will seek death but will not find it; they will long to die, but death will flee from them." (Apocalypse 9:8)

The Great Resurrection by Wilhelm Lehmbruck (1913) focuses on the resurrection of the female body. The bodies here are spirits; there is a thin line between body and spirit. This scene is more hopeful.

"And I heard a voice from heaven saying, 'Write this: Blessed are the dead who from now on die in the Lord.' 'Yes,' says the Spirit, 'they will rest from their labors, for their deeds follow them.'" (Apocalypse 14:13)

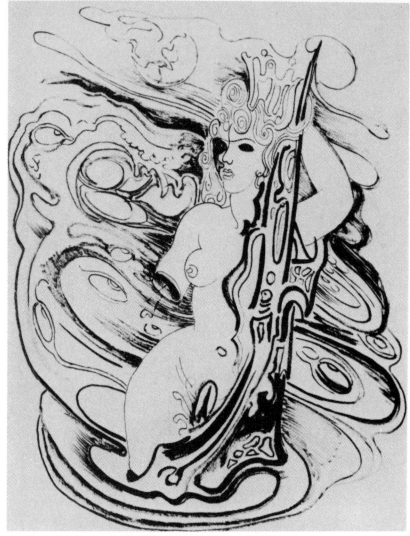

Rudolf Schlichter's *The Shipwrecked Culture* (1948) is from a series on the Apocalypse reflecting postwar Germany. An erotic female torso stares darkly, while apparently holding a gun. Culture is presented as immoral and aggressive, led by a female. The image is meant to arouse. The message is ambiguous: the masculine gaze has led to destruction. But why is it that, as in the Apocalypse, a sexually powerful female leads men to desire, and ultimately, to death?

"Let anyone who has an ear listen: If you are to be taken captive, into captivity you go; if you kill with the sword, with the sword you must be killed. Here is a call for the endurance and faith of the saints."

(Apocalypse 13:9-10)

"Neither culture nor its destruction is erotic; it is the seam between them, the fault, the flaw which becomes so." — Roland Barthes